Praise for
WHO I AM

Who I Am: The Man Behind the Badge is a real live look into the life experiences and sacrifices of a front line street cop and later homicide sergeant in South Florida during the turbulent 1980's, 90's, and into the new century.

We follow Officer Shaw as he begins his law enforcement career as a young naïve trainee, then as a rookie officer with all the normal doubts and fears; developing into a seasoned experienced officer, and finishing his career as a decorated, hardened, and somewhat cynical homicide sergeant.

You will not be able to put this book down as you follow the author through his career call by call experiencing in raw, graphic, and gut wrenching language what would become a normal day for him and members of a police department during this time period. You will never look at a Law Enforcement Officer the same again...

So slide into a patrol car, buckle up, and prepare yourself for the realities of Law Enforcement and the ride of your life.

—Retired Deputy Chief Edward L. Beyer, Jr.
Hialeah Police Department

Written by a seasoned police veteran of a major police force, it doesn't get more real than this. Gritty, gut-wrenching, and intensely personal, this is a must read for anyone in law enforcement, contemplating a career in law enforcement, or has a loved one in law enforcement. This book shines a glaring spotlight on some of the many reasons every citizen should back the blue.

—Patricia L. Diaz
U.S. federal prosecutor (ret.) and wife of a retired homicide detective

I was unprepared for the realities of what our police officers do day to day. That in spite of their personal turmoil, they always answer that next call, that next alert.

This is a revealing and detailed read for anyone who has a friend or family member in law enforcement. I have a new respect to the dedication and sacrifice of those who put on the badge every day.

—Michael Jimison
Vietnam Helicopter Pilots Association (VHPA)

WHO I AM

WHO I AM

THE MAN BEHIND THE BADGE

Jeff Shaw

Mountain Arbor
Press
Alpharetta, GA

The author has tried to recreate events, locations, and conversations from his/her memories of them. In some instances, in order to maintain their anonymity, the author has changed the names of individuals and places. He/she may also have changed some identifying characteristics and details such as physical attributes, occupations, and places of residence. The author has made every effort to give credit to the source of any images, quotes, or other material contained within and obtain permissions when feasible.

ISBN: 978-1-63183-747-0 – Softcover
ISBN: 978-1-63183-748-7 – ePub
ISBN: 978-1-63183-749-4 – Mobi

Library of Congress Control Number: 2019920984

Printed in the United States of America 0 1 0 6 2 0

∞This paper meets the requirements of ANSI/NISO Z39.48-1992 (Permanence of Paper)

To Susan, who has always been more than my wife. She is the lighthouse in my storm.

"Sometimes we are just the collateral damage in someone else's war against themselves."

–Lauren Eden

Contents

FOREWORD

Jeff Shaw is a survivor. There was no need of him making this revelation upon our first meeting—his demeanor made it clear. He grabbed my attention because he kept his back to the wall upon entering the reception area, his eyes quickly evaluating the room's occupants.

Immediately impressed, I wondered: Who is this dude? Introductions were made and then we settled down to business. I stepped to the microphone; Jeff sat up front, off to the right, within easy reach of an ancillary door. Which piqued my curiosity even more, prompting me to think I needed to know more about this man.

Ours was a writer's conference. The usual fare of would-be authors chasing the dream of hitting the jackpot, hopefully discovering the secrets to winning the literary lottery and its grand prize of having produced a New York Times best-seller. Learning from guest speakers—all of whom were highly successful authors—the ways and means of making the gigantic leap from simply tossing random words onto a blank page to that of composing a manuscript of quality.

Unlike the other newbies in attendance, Jeff did not appear intimidated by the moment. Nervous, yes. But not intimidated. At first glance, what captivated me most about him were those eyes—which loudly spoke of an accumulation of fatigue and grief. Eyes that had seen too much, too often. Eyes that tried, yet failed, to be masked by the even-tempered smile that accompanied him.

I'm in the habit of reading people. It's kept me alive. Admittedly, I took an immediate liking of Jeff Shaw, for not only did he ask intelligent questions over the next few days, but he also carried himself in an easygoing manner. His humility was not feigned. Knowing there were no easy answers to the journey upon which he was now embarking, it was obvious he wanted to learn.

Yes, his eyes told me as much. The eyes of a combat veteran, that was my assumption. Someone who'd been there, done that, and had a story or two to tell. I wondered aloud if he was Army or Marines.

"I was a cop, a police officer in South Florida; served twenty-four years at the Hialeah Police Department," Jeff said. And immediately my gut was gripped by an invisible fist. He need not tell me anything more.

One of my daughters is a police officer. So is her husband. Both have been on the job for almost two decades. Each carry a gun wherever they go. As veteran police officers such as Jeff Shaw will tell you, "that gun that has only one purpose—a purpose that is always in the back of their mind, because their career path is dealing in death."

My daughter stops by the house two, three times a week. She's verbal; she talks, I listen. Her husband is more private; he drives to the mountains on his days off, running the trails at random. Two different ways of releasing tension, unloading the crushing weight that comes with the job—of excising the daily accumulation of mental fatigue. Releasing tension, which helps keep them sane. For the time being.

Yet the exorcism is never complete.

As cop-turned-author Jeff Shaw says in *Who I Am: The Man Behind the Badge,* "Such is the price one pays for being a police officer, putting their life on the line every day."

That statement is about as close to braggadocio as Jeff gets. His story is that of every man or woman who steps into the uniform and pins the police officer's badge on their left breast. Those who spend much of their lifetime dealing in death, dreading the dispatcher's call: "3-30 in progress, shots fired . . . subjects are still on the scene, armed with shotguns and machine guns—multiple victims down."

Having compiled a case book of vignettes, he gives the reader an up-close-and-personal look at what cops nationwide experience every day—a glimpse into society's horrific underbelly of spousal abuse, fatal automobile accidents, suicides, ethnic riots, and gangbanger vendettas.

Unlike the glamorized police fare served up on television, the stories he shares are void of self-serving heroism. Instead, his depiction of the blood and guts and abject terror of the job is accompanied by humble self-evaluations.

Stories such as the time he was a one-ounce-trigger-pull away from killing an 18-year-old non-English-speaking Hispanic kid holding a replica Smith & Wesson .45—a weapon which proved to be a pellet gun.

Stories about fellow officers he helped bury, friends killed in the line of duty.

Stories about PTSD, how wife Susan was his "safety net," helping take care of his mental well-being.

Stories about random and unexplainable death—a man and his date are dining at a crowded restaurant when a stranger gets up from a nearby table and plunges a steak knife into the man's back and simply walks away. The victim looks at his date and says, "He stabbed me!", then collapsed and died.

Did Jeff ever kill anyone while on the job? No.

But despite having retired in 2003, his dreams still have a

rough edge to them: "I'm in a desperate gun battle and either my gun won't fire or I'm out of ammunition. Or I'm negotiating with someone holding my children and wife hostage."

Nonetheless, he says, "I wouldn't have traded my career for anything."

I am here not only to applaud Jeff Shaw's career path but also to thank him for his service.

As you are about to see, his is a story well worth sharing.

–Jedwin Smith
Former U.S. Marine and war correspondent
for the *Atlanta Journal-Constitution*
Twice nominated for the Pulitzer Prize
Author: Our Brother's Keeper
Fatal Treasure
Let's Get It On!
I Am Israel

PREFACE

"Life is pleasant. Death is peaceful. It's the transition that's troublesome."

–Isaac Asimov

Most people have never seen a dead person, other than a loved one at a funeral home. I've been to many funerals, and I always look around the room—I study you. Some of you won't approach the casket even if it's closed. Some cross themselves as protection from something the dead may possess, or to simply ask the Lord to accept their friend or loved one into heaven. Some stand in the back of the room talking to people they don't know, just to be as far away as possible from the death inside that coffin. Some never look at the deceased's face, not even a quick glance, because the dead are so…dead.

Some thank God they only have to experience death once or twice in their life when an aunt, an uncle, or their parents pass away, and the experience is, of course, very emotional, as it should be.

But the death I have dealt with is much different. In a funeral home, the deceased are always clean, their hair is perfect, they're wearing their best clothes, and there are no smells, no screaming, and no blood—just the empty shell of a human being. We call it passing away, or he's moved on, or he's in a better place. We avoid saying they're dead, but let's face it—they are dead. The dead aren't pretty—and their deaths—the acts of dying, are much worse.

Yes, death has a different meaning for us in law enforcement.

We deal with death in one form or another every day: homicides, suicides, accidental deaths, and natural deaths. Who is the first person to respond when someone finds granny dead in the morning? We do, and we often find them in horrible places, deformed with rigor mortis, and in pools of their own vomit or blood. We comfort their family, then it's off to our next call.

We carry a gun everywhere we go—and that gun has only one purpose—a purpose that is always in the back of our minds.

Few people will ever see a gunshot wound in real life. They will never apply pressure to a knife wound to keep someone from bleeding to death—and fail.

It's what you signed up for. It's what we pay you for.

I've heard it all, and yes, it is what we signed up for, but that doesn't make it any easier or any less traumatic. We spend our entire career, a majority of our lifetime—dealing in death.

In *Who I Am: The Man Behind the Badge,* I'm going to describe all the gore and all the horrors and all the emotions I felt, not to gross you out but to let you know what I experienced.

I'm the worst bullshitter in America, so I've done my best to write these scenes exactly as they occurred and as accurately as possible. I've withheld the names of most individuals to protect their identity. I've also withheld certain aspects of some scenes because there are people still in prison for these crimes.

If you find any of these stories disturbing or uncomfortable, then I have accomplished my goal—because I was equally disturbed and uncomfortable.

And I live with these memories every day.

CHAPTER 1

WHY NOW?

I retired from law enforcement in 2003 at the age of 50. Why write this memoir now?

Who I Am: The Man Behind the Badge started ten years ago when I wanted my kids to understand who their father was, and why I was so different than other fathers. Why did I say no when other fathers said yes, why did I pry into their personal lives when other parents didn't, and why was I so strict?

I also wanted my friends and the rest of my family to know what I saw, the things I did and how I felt about them, and how they affect me now.

I also was worried as the years went by I would forget the details of the scenes, and they would be lost forever. As much as I often wish I was freed from these memories, it would mean forgetting the victims, forgetting friends who were lost. Somehow I would feel less proud of my career; after all, I survived these horrors when others didn't.

I'm an ass sometimes. I mistrust people—I assume the worst in them, and they must prove to me they are worthy of friendship. For all those years I met the worst society had to offer: rapists, murderers, drug addicts, and thieves. It's often easier for me to avoid meeting people. I've become antisocial. I know it, and I accept it, and I wish I could be a better person.

So I wonder, was I born this way? Or is it the people I've met, the things I've seen, or the things I've done that have made me who I am?

I worked for twenty-four years at the Hialeah Police Department. In the 1980s, Hialeah was the third-largest city in Florida, and in the 2018 United States census, Hialeah ranks in at number six.

I began with a story I titled *The Right Place #2*, the story of saving a life. Each of the stories that followed was a life-changing event. As I wrote, I began to realize just how horrific some of my memories were, and there were so many of them. I thought, if I can remember them so clearly, they must have had a significant effect on me, even though I didn't always realize it at the time.

My wife read the first few and cried, and after all these years I still cry, too. I sat back and realized how profound some of them were, and I wanted to share them with my fellow retirees, to see if they remembered them.

When I typed the first word, my intended readers weren't my fellow police officers or combat veterans. I'm sure they have seen everything I have and worse, but the more I wrote and began describing these events to my author friends and to my fellow retired police officers, the more I knew these stories had a purpose. First, I learned that these officers suffer from memories just like I do, and secondly, I learned most people have no clue what an officer does every day.

So as I wrote, I wrote knowing these fellow officers would be reading how I cope, or sometimes fail to cope, with my depression and anger. How talking about it lightens the load I carry every day. And maybe reading *Who I Am* will lighten their load, too.

Lastly, I wanted to give everyone else a vivid picture of what those of us in law enforcement do, not what they may see on TV, not what they see in a Hollywood movie, but what really happens on the street.

CHAPTER 2

PTSD

Some people I've talked to say I suffer from PTSD.

When I think of PTSD, I think of the movie *Saving Private Ryan*. I see the soldiers running to the beach, being cut down and slaughtered by machine gun fire; I see them returning from war with missing arms and legs, burnt and blinded by combat. To me, they have the *right* to suffer from post-traumatic stress disorder. I look at myself in the mirror, and I'm unmarked. I am whole and healthy, at least on the outside.

I consider myself a smart man, and I can rationalize my own symptoms, my emotions, and those of the people around me. I took psychology in college; I attended various classes and schools including Hostage Negotiations at Miami-Dade County's Police Training Institute where I learned how to talk to someone suffering from psychological trauma and how to negotiate with the violent and the insane people I dealt with on the street.

I learned to read people, to diagnose their body language, the things they said, and things we call "tells" when they lied. I spent weeks in classrooms then years of putting that psychology to use on the street. So I can see the signs and symptoms—in others and in myself.

A friend of mine wrote, "Normal people have an occasional nightmare…" He is a Marine who served in Beirut and then as a war correspondent in Africa, and I knew exactly what he was saying in those few simple words.

You see, I have nightmares every night, and when I'm lucky, it's only one or two. I often dream I'm in a desperate gun battle and either my gun won't fire or I'm out of ammunition. Or I'm negotiating with someone holding my children and wife hostage.

The dreams aren't always about the job, but they all involve some life-threatening event, a theme of desperation so intense I wake up startled at four in the morning, drenched in sweat, and I feel like I'm having a heart attack, and there is no going back to sleep after that.

Some of the comments people have made to me over the years give me the impression they thought I was somehow a victim, and I probably regretted having lived through those times. But that's not the case. In a way, I cherish those memories; I saw and did things many people can only dream about. But along with the memories, I carry a little baggage around with me. So as you read this, don't feel sorry for me. I wouldn't have traded this career for anything.

I also wrote this story to help people understand that the cops they see driving down the street (and I) are different than they are—not better, but different. I hope the next time they see a patrol car at a donut shop, their first thought won't be some fat and lazy cop is getting fatter on their tax dollars.

CHAPTER 3

DEPRESSION

I didn't go to the bar to socialize that night—I went there to drink.

It was the summer of 1990. I had the night off. I wasn't dating anyone, I had a career in law enforcement that was going nowhere, I was suffering from insomnia, and when I could sleep I was having nightmares. My doctor had prescribed Dalmane, a heavy sleep medication, and the side effects included feelings of paranoia and suicidal ideation. As I looked around the bar, I realized I was also the oldest person there. Depressed, alone, and wallowing in self-pity, I went home.

I found myself sitting on my bed, cradling my service .45. As I held the gun in both hands, I was thinking of ending a conflict—like deciding to have a root canal after months of suffering a toothache.

I studied every etched and engraved word and number on that gun.

Smith and Wesson.

Model 645.

Made in the U.S.A.

I felt how powerful it was. How deadly. And I put it back in my gun belt.

I knew I had come close to pulling the trigger.

It was a lethal combination of alcohol, depression, and most importantly, no longer fearing death. Yet somehow, the rational side of my brain took over and kicked the emotional side to the curb. That's all I can think of—I made a rational decision that night, and I never held my gun like that again.

***

The International Association of Chiefs of Police reports that more law enforcement officers die by suicide than are killed in the line of duty, and *Mental Health Daily* reports that law enforcement officers are ranked number three in the professions most likely to commit suicide.

We in law enforcement see so many deaths that its mystery and fear become less significant. The blackness of death fades to subtle gray, and all too often it becomes a muted light, beckoning us. Death becomes an alternative other people are too terrified to consider.

Fortunately for me, months later I began dating the woman who would become my wife, Susan, and things changed for the better.

For a police officer suffering from depression, there wasn't, and probably still isn't, anyone to confide in, no place they could seek help without ending their career. We had an officer assigned as a grief counselor, one that we were supposed to be able to speak to if we were having issues like depression. In reality, there was never an option of telling someone, even a friend at work, and I never did. The few officers who did mention depression were taken off the road and put into what we called "The Rubber Gun Squad," a desk assignment, and most remained there for the rest of their career.

So I was one of the lucky ones. I had Susan, and she was the safety net I needed. Susan was a police dispatcher and knew how to listen and when to offer advice. She understood the stress of working in law enforcement that many others' loved ones don't.

I didn't always have to tell her about my shift—she seemed to know. Maybe someone called her at home and said, "Jeff was just involved in a shooting, or Jeff was just in a bad accident," or maybe she could just read it in my face.

So I was lucky, but far too many aren't. I lived to retire 13 years later.

***

Months after retiring, I began to realize how different I was, and not in a good way. I worried I suffered from some form of social anxiety and I pushed people away. I never looked forward to the holidays like everyone else and for some reason, the holidays depressed me and still do. So I often wonder, what is wrong with me?

I dislike meeting new people, and I hate going out anywhere where I know I will be among strangers. It's a feeling that began several years after I became an officer. I would walk into a crowded room, whether it was a New Year's Eve party, a bar, or even a shopping mall—anywhere I was surrounded by non-cops.

It's not like cops are fun to be with, but I just didn't seem to fit in with other people. I'd be introduced to some stranger, and as everyone smiled and made small talk, I would be thinking to myself—*Does he abuse his wife? Does he molest his neighbor's kids? Is he a drug addict? Does she hate cops because she couldn't talk her way out of a speeding ticket two years ago?*

I was at a wedding reception recently and I had one of those moments. I was introduced to a guy, a friend of someone I was sitting next to, and the alarm bells went off. It has been sixteen years and I can still spot them.

This guy's eyes were bouncing all over the room as he spoke to me, but he never looked me in the eye. He was talking a little too fast, a little overconfident—and I didn't believe a word he said. A drug addict talks and acts like that, a pathological liar talks like that, and often they are both. They can have a needle in their arm and try and convince you they are clean and sober.

Some might say I'm just a cynic, which may be, but I have been around these people for most of my life.

It took a long time for me to warm up to people and this continues today, not as bad as it used to be, but I still feel it, and I know *they* feel it as well.

Have you heard the term the holiday blues? Many people suffer from this affliction, and I know how hard it is on my wife and family. I would dread the approach of Thanksgiving and feel a huge relief once January 1st was in the rearview mirror. Why?

As I'm typing right now, it's the first week of January 2018, and this holiday season was a bad one. Family issues this time and I can't say more. So what depresses me during this joyful time of the year?

To start with, I had to work most holidays. It took me ten years to get the seniority for weekends off, and once I was promoted, it took me another ten years to regain any seniority. Seniority is important in a profession that works 24/7 and unless you were a senior officer, you worked weekends and holidays on the midnight shift.

While my family and loved ones sat down to dinner, I dealt

with an increase in crime, violence, and other people's depression because suicides spike during the holiday season. Occasionally a holiday would fall on my day off but most of my family would celebrate the holiday on the weekend, so again, I dealt with crime, death, and all the crap associated with it.

Some days it felt like I was playing in the sewer while my friends and family were at Disney World.

There is a new phenomenon similar to the holiday blues—the social media blues. Think about Facebook or Instagram posts, where friends are smiling, taking selfies, and posting beautiful pictures of their kids and grandchildren, they're playing at the beach or on vacation, out at restaurants with other friends, or having drinks and dancing.

But some people are at home. They are depressed, and they wonder: how is it possible everyone they know is happy, and they are in misery? And their depression spirals out of control.

Chapter 4

The Rookie Years

I wanted a career in aviation. I had a pilot's license, and I had learned to paint small planes at Opa-Locka Airport. But Vietnam was winding down, and the job market was flooded with pilots and mechanics coming home from the war. Instead, my first significant job was working for Ranch House restaurants. I had just started my senior year of high school and worked after school as a busboy with Billy Bird, my friend since second grade. I worked on and off for Ranch House over the years as a cook, and eventually, I became the manager of three stores in North Miami.

Many Hialeah police officers ate dinner at Ranch House, and I knew a few of them by name. Late at night, some would come in for coffee, and I would join them at the counter if I wasn't busy. Many nights I sat with Jim McKeown; Jim was a K-9 sergeant with the department, and his daughter and my sister were close friends.

"You should put in an application," Jim said one night. "The department has a test in a few weeks."

I had thought of applying more than once, but I never thought I was man enough. Looking back I suppose I was an introvert, drifting along and trying to find my way. But I found the idea of being in law enforcement exciting and Jim saw that.

"I think I will," I said.

So at the age of 26, the City of Hialeah hired me as a police recruit, and I started the academy in September of 1979.

Jim was alive when I wrote the paragraph above, but he passed away soon after. He was a good man, and he was one of the supervisors I tried to emulate when I was promoted. I hope I was at least half the sergeant he was.

My first two days on the job were spent getting equipment: shirts, pants, socks, those shiny patent leather shoes, a gun belt, an under belt, a holster, handcuffs, and a gun, of course. At the time, Hialeah, like most departments, restricted its officers to a .38-caliber revolver with a four-inch barrel. I bought a nickel-plated Smith and Wesson Model 19.

I mention the type of gun because I've found people are fascinated by guns. At one time I probably was, too, but soon it became just a tool, no different than a flashlight or a pair of handcuffs.

The first day at the academy was a memory impossible to forget. I woke at four in the morning, dressed, and stood in front of the mirror to double-check my uniform and shine the brass belt buckle. I'd already heard horror stories about the daily uniform inspections from others who had been through it. I had worn uniforms before, Boy Scouts uniforms of all things, but this was going to be different. Although the shirt material was baby blue, the color of a trainee, it also said Hialeah Police on the shoulder patch. It was a big moment, and as I looked in that mirror, I felt my life changing.

I thought I was ready, and I arrived at the academy before sunrise, scared shitless.

The 24-week police academy was part of the Miami-Dade Junior College in Dade County. Most all departments sent their police trainees there, and I saw several hundred of us milling about the campus. It was clear they were forming into groups, and I eventually found mine.

The groups were made up of BLEs, or Basic Law Enforcement classes, and I was in BLE 42. There were 26 of us in this BLE, and the majority were from the city of Miami. There were also trainees from Hollywood, Homestead, Hialeah Gardens, Virginia Gardens, Miami Springs, and two of us from Hialeah.

Our instructors, or training advisors as they were called, had us form up in rows, squads, and platoons: a formation we had to memorize and repeat every day. Three days a week we lined up for uniform inspection and the other two days a week we lined up for physical training or PT.

We learned to march in this formation and how to salute and how to respect the flag; we had squad leaders, platoon leaders, a class leader, and finally, the training advisors.

"Why do police officers need to know how to march?" I wondered as I sweltered in the hot sun those first few weeks.

I had serious doubts at times: What have I put myself into? I want this job, but am I worthy? I struggled with this last thought every day: "Am I worthy of the position? Can I be a good police officer?"

During the first week we began defensive tactics instruction in the gym and a physical ability test where we were weighed, did as many push-ups, sit-ups, etc., as we could, and the results were recorded. I was 5′11″ and weighed 138 pounds. I felt too small and too skinny; there were others shorter and lighter, but it still left me self-conscious. I passed each test, but some just barely.

I decided during those first few weeks that I was going to change. I was going to do everything I could to get stronger, to run farther and faster, and I did. I ran at home on the weekends. I lifted weights, drank protein drinks, and tried to eat better.

As the weeks progressed, I noticed during our morning one-mile run that I was passing more cadets. I was no longer bringing up the rear but running in the middle of the pack. By the time I graduated, I finally felt comfortable in a police uniform. I felt worthy.

In the first few weeks, we had firearms training. This was merely firing at a silhouette target without any stress. We fired approximately 2,000 rounds in five days. It was designed to eliminate the few people who were incapable of learning to fire a weapon and hit their target. We lost a few people, even with another week of one-on-one personal training.

Months later, we had module two of firearms training. Another 40 hour course but it was at night, and they added stress: flashing red and blue strobe lights, sirens blaring, instructors and other recruits screaming insults, a taped radio transmission of a catastrophic event blasting out through loudspeakers—all of this simulated firing while under attack. One trainee shot herself in the leg because she pulled the trigger before her gun was out of its holster. It was a grazing wound down the outside of her thigh. After she healed, she retook module two and eventually graduated with us.

That week I learned how stress affected my performance and I learned how to manage it. I learned to tune it out and let my training guide me.

The first day of the third week we attended an autopsy at Jackson Memorial Hospital. The autopsy was scheduled early in our training to weed out anyone who had doubts about their ability to see the gore associated with death.

We could smell the dead as soon as we got out of our cars. As we walked into the Dade County morgue, an older section of the hospital, we saw dozens of stainless steel gurneys lined up against the walls. Some had bodies on them, and one of the bodies was really small—a child. I told myself to think of them as mannequins, and I tried not to look too closely at the rest.

The medical examiner walked us up to our body and we stood in a circle, just a few feet away from the man. He was a thin, athletic-looking African American in his thirties who had fallen into a lake and drowned—and he was "fresh," only a day or two had passed since his death.

The examiner started with the "Y" incision on his chest, just like the crime shows on TV. There was no blood. We learned the body doesn't bleed without the blood pressure supplied by a beating heart, and this man's heart hadn't beaten in days. Still, the blood is all there; it's just trapped in the major blood vessels.

As the scalpel sliced through flesh, we saw a thin layer of yellow fat. The layer of fat varies according to the deceased's body size, the examiner explained. It looked just like chicken fat, and under the fat was the red meat of muscle.

Using a device that looked like a cross between bolt cutters and tree pruning shears, the examiner cut through the breastbone, or sternum, making a crunching sound similar to lopping off a tree branch. Placing his hands into the chest cavity, the examiner removed each organ one at a time, weighed and dissected it, then put it in a big bucket lined with a plastic bag.

As the examiner removed an organ, a lung, for example, he

explained some of the things he looked for, whether or not the organ appeared healthy, did the victim smoke, and were there any signs of cancer?

Finally, the examiner sliced the scalp from the back of the head and pulled it forward until it covered the man's face. Using an electric saw similar to the Dremel tool, the examiner made a complete circular cut around the skull. Smoke and steam rose from the blade, and the smell of burning flesh was pungent. I was too close to the stench, and I had to move away. He took a small plastic mallet and tapped on the skull cap. The bone came off in one piece—and the brain slid out. When they saw the brain lying next to the empty skull, several of my fellow cadets had to leave the room.

After he examined the brain for defects, he put everything except the intestines in a clear bag, placed the organs back inside the chest cavity, and sewed the man up. He explained that the bacteria in intestines would wreak havoc on the body and the onset of decay would be swift, making funeral arrangements difficult, so those intestines, or the gut, as he called it, are incinerated.

The examiner pulled the scalp back over the skull, stitched it in place, and the man looked like he was ready for his funeral, all clean and, except for the sutures holding him together, asleep.

Several more of the cadets had to leave the room. I coped by looking away and trying to think of other things every time I thought I would puke—which was often. However, I couldn't block out the sounds and the smells. Later, I felt pretty good about making it through the entire autopsy.

A full autopsy is done for criminal cases and suspicious or unnatural deaths, such as the accidental drowning of the man above. Under normal circumstances, as when someone's eighty-

or ninety-year-old grandfather passes away, a doctor will usually sign the death certificate, and there will be no autopsy.

***

One of my training advisors was Sergeant Robert Yee, who worked for the city of Miami. Sergeant Yee had been assigned to the academy after being shot in the line of duty, probably as a way to help ease him back into the job.

Soon after our class graduated Sergeant Yee went back to regular duties with the city of Miami and would eventually be promoted to captain before retiring in the mid-1990s. In July of 2009, he was shot and killed while working as a private security officer at a Miami River marina. The gunman was arrested and convicted in 2016, and the investigation was featured on the television show, *The First 48 Hours*.

Sergeant Yee was an intelligent, professional, and friendly man. Rest in peace, Sergeant!

The class graduated in February of 1980, and I spent the next two months riding with field training officers or FTOs.

The first month, I rode on day shift. I was a true rookie in every sense of the word. The officer, Walt, was a veteran, and I learned a lot from him.

Working day shift, I found officers wrote a lot of reports. Businesses are open and reporting thefts or burglaries, people awaken to find someone has stolen their car during the night, etc.

There were also a lot of domestic violence calls, and I found myself—only 26 years old, never married, no children, very few meaningful relationships—in some stranger's house, trying to help them solve their family's crisis.

I felt very uncomfortable on each one and that feeling lasted the entire month. The other calls were easy to deal with, and soon I felt competent writing reports and handling most of the situations we were dispatched to.

The next month I rode with another FTO on the afternoon shift. This officer and the types of calls we handled could not have been more different. When it gets dark, shit happens! That was the saying, and it was true. I saw things that shocked me and things that a classroom could never prepare me for, and I knew I had a lot to learn if I wanted to live through them.

I was involved in my first car chase, my first foot chase, stabbings, rapes, and armed robberies, often in dark and deserted streets.

I learned officer survival skills, things I had never thought of before, like how to sit while driving so the door post provides a few inches of protection from a bullet, how to carry a second weapon, why I needed to carry a knife, and how to patrol and what to look for when the sun went down.

One night we were dispatched to my first murder. I might have been on other homicides, but never at the actual crime scene, as I was most likely holding an outside perimeter. All crime scenes have some type of perimeter; sometimes it can take twenty officers and be the size of an entire city block, or like this call, just me and my FTO in an open field keeping spectators and the media from contaminating everything.

This next story, "The Philips-Head Screwdriver," was that homicide, and it was an eye-opener for me.

Chapter 5

The Phillips-Head Screwdriver

I had no idea how I would feel when I had to kneel down and touch my first murder victim.

One night my training partner and I were dispatched to a disturbance in an open field, "men fighting," the dispatcher said. I was still nervous. I had been out of the academy only a month, and every call had an element of danger and excitement.

I was behind the wheel and probably terrified. I tried to picture what I would see and prepare myself for what we would find. Would it be two men fighting or would it be twenty men? Would they be armed, and with what?

When we arrived, the field was pitch-black, there were no signs of a fight, and there were no men anywhere. I breathed a sigh of relief.

In the beam of my flashlight, all I saw were waist-high brown weeds.

My FTO and I got out of the car and began looking through the tall weeds. I had a cheap flashlight, a Kel-Lite, but it was still bright enough to ruin my night vision—it created tunnel vision, and I could see only what was right in front of me.

Not far into the weeds we found a young man lying supine—a fancy way of saying he was flat on his back, and he was clearly dead. But I knelt down anyway and put my fingers on his neck to check for a pulse. It was creepy touching a dead man; he was still warm, but he was definitely dead.

Sticking out of his chest was the handle of a Craftsman Phillips-head screwdriver.

As I knelt over him, I thought, I have that same exact screwdriver in my garage at home. It had a clear plastic handle with a blue stripe, and I could see #2 Phillips USA on the side. I couldn't see any part of the shaft; it was sunk deep into his chest, all the way up to the blue striped handle.

As I knelt over this young dead man, who was probably alive just twenty minutes earlier, I couldn't help but think about who he was or what had he been doing just moments before he was stabbed with the screwdriver. Was he a father? Was he a criminal? I never heard one way or another as once the detectives arrived, it was on to our next call.

That's the way it was. There was never a moment to think about the call, it was always on to the next one, and I needed to be fully focused on what it was I was doing right then, not thirty minutes ago.

This was my first up close and personal homicide, and it happened a hundred yards away from the Sayonara Bar, where I will have a terrifying call one month later.

Chapter 6

Rose

I met Rose one afternoon while I was still riding with Eddie, my second field training officer.

We were dispatched to a vandalism call, and as the dispatcher read the address, Eddie smiled and said, "This will be a good one for you."

A middle-aged woman was standing in the front yard waiting for us. She was in her late fifties and in average shape for a woman her age. Medium height, medium build, medium brown hair—average. She was wearing a wig, which was a shade redder than the brown hair underneath it.

The house was a blue one-story stucco, CBS (concrete block structure) home that looked identical to all the other homes on the street. The only thing unusual about it was every jalousie window was cranked wide-open. I say it was unusual because in South Florida, most people have the windows shut tight because their air conditioners were running at maximum.

Eddie introduced me to Rose as we went inside the house, then Rose explained why she called.

"They came again last night," she said, pointing to the dust in several corners of the house. "Look what they left this time."

I looked, and all I saw was a terrazzo floor that hadn't been swept in a long time, with dust and dirt that had accumulated around the baseboards.

"They all raped me again, too."

That got my attention. Rape is a long way from vandalism. I looked at Eddie for some guidance, and he had the same mischievous smile on his face.

"Who raped you?" I asked.

"The neighbors—and their wives too. They gassed me last night, and when I woke up, I saw all this dirt."

I looked around the house trying to understand what she was saying. Was this a prank, were my fellow officers playing a joke on the rookie? Or had I missed something? I looked at Eddy again and realized he was enjoying my dilemma as I tried to figure it out.

"Rose," Eddie said, "I think I can help you."

Eddie asked her to take off her wig, and I saw it was lined with aluminum foil.

"Stand still," he said. Eddie rotated the squelch nob on his radio, causing a hiss of static, then he turned the volume to maximum, held up the hissing radio next to Rose, and circled it around her head several times.

"You'll be okay now," Eddie said.

Rose followed us out to our car, smiling.

I was called to her home a dozen times over the years and ran into her on the street as well.

On one of the calls she said she had been raped again, this time by people who had landed a ship on her roof. She showed me zigzag cracks in the stucco she said were a result of the weight of a massive ship, as she called it, and wanted a report. Most homes in South Florida were made from this CBS block, and the zigzag pattern in the stucco or plaster was common.

Again the windows were cranked wide-open, "to get the sleeping gas out," she said. I asked her if aliens had landed on her roof, and she smiled and said, "I'm not crazy."

Another time I was sent to assist a woman who was trapped in a bingo hall after the business had closed. It was near midnight, the building was dark, and the doors were locked tight. I knocked on the glass door and pressed my face against the glass to see inside. Mostly what I saw was my own reflection.

Then I noticed it wasn't just my face I was looking at—another face was pressed against the glass on the other side, looking back at me. It scared the crap out of me, and I knew immediately it was Rose.

"Get me out of here!" she yelled.

Rose said she had been playing bingo when she needed to use the bathroom. While on the toilet, someone had slipped sleeping gas under the stall, and it knocked her out.

"I'm sure they all raped me," she said. "When I came to, it was dark, and the doors were locked."

I called the emergency contact number for the hall, and someone came out to unlock the door.

There were never any signs Rose had been raped; in fact, it was the other things she wanted investigated: the dirt on her floors, the cracks in her walls, etc. She never appeared a danger to herself or a threat to anyone else. She had family nearby who checked on her regularly. She was delusional but not to a point she couldn't function in society.

I often saw Rose walking up and down one of the main streets in Hialeah. Usually, her reddish wig was a little crooked, and I could see her brown hair and the aluminum foil sticking out of it. She would always wave when she recognized me.

Although I knew other officers had spoken to her family and she was being taken care of, I always felt a little sad for Rose.

CHAPTER 7

ON MY OWN

After five months of being in the academy and two months of riding with training officers, one night I found myself alone in a patrol car for the first time. It was 10:30. I sat behind the wheel and loaded five rounds of double-aught buckshot into a worn-out Mossberg 12-gauge shotgun and locked it into the vertical rack. I jammed my handheld radio into its charger and prepared to go into service. I listened as my fellow midnight shift officers began checking in, hoping my voice wouldn't crack, knowing it probably would.

The empty passenger seat was huge and terrifying.

Years before when I was taking flying lessons, my instructor and I were practicing touch- and-go landings, and as I was about to touch down, he said, "Come to a complete stop at the end of the runway and let me out."

The next takeoff was terrifying—and so was the next landing.

Driving out of the police station alone felt equally terrifying, but I keyed the microphone and said I was 09, in-service.

I was in-service and I was alone.

We worked ten-hour shifts four days a week, and the midnight shift was from 10 p.m. to 8 a.m. Our shift overlapped with the afternoon shift. The overlap gave the city two full shifts for about four hours during the roughest part of the night. In 1980, that average was twenty-eight officers.

Two calls during those first few days on my own stand out.

The first was a domestic violence call on my very first night. This was a time in police work when domestic violence and the rights of abused women were becoming a national issue. We spent many hours in the classroom and in role model training scenarios, learning to defuse and document domestic violence calls—and the importance of making an arrest when warranted.

I was assigned as the primary officer and an afternoon shift officer was my backup. I began mentally preparing myself as I drove to the apartment building. As I parked, I met not just my backup officer, but his zone partner as well. Being a rookie, I didn't know these officers very well, but we made small talk on the way up the elevator, then I knocked on the door.

A young woman opened the door.

"My husband slapped me," she said.

Her eye was swollen, and her lip was bruised and bleeding. I heard a man yelling in another room.

The woman explained she and her husband had had an argument, and he had hit her in the face.

Before I could speak, the backup officer said, "Ma'am, this is a civil matter, and you should go to the State Attorney's office if you want him arrested."

The next thing I knew, we were going down the elevator, and the two offficers were talking to each other. I was worried about the legal ramifications. I had been assigned to this call and was responsible.

"Shouldn't we have arrested him?" I asked.

"This is how it really works, forget all that academy stuff."

The officer told the dispatcher to show him handling the call. "Show me 09 (in-service), no report."

This relieved me of some of the legal burdens—or so I hoped.

In the old days, before I graduated, the woman would have been the victim of a simple battery, one that required an officer to witness firsthand before he could make an arrest. But the laws had changed in the last year or so and domestic violence was now an exception to that rule, and the husband should have been arrested.

So much for all those hours of training, I thought. From then on, I did, however, make it a point to always make an arrest for domestic violence when the call warranted it.

The second call was just a few days later, at the Sayonara Bar.

Chapter 8

The Sayonara Bar

I had been to the Sayonara Bar several times during my training; it was a rough, Hispanic bar known to be a hangout for one of the most violent Colombian drug cartels in South Florida, and I had already worked one homicide there while I was still in training. I spoke to a friend of mine who was working that night. He remembered hearing the call being dispatched and thinking it was probably BS...until he heard my voice on the radio.

I still have one of those flashbulb memories when I think of this call—like a photograph, I can hold it up and see everything in the picture.

It was April 7th, 1980, and my shift had started at 10 p.m. I had been on the road for less than an hour when the alert tone came over the radio. The alert tone was meant to do just that: alert officers a serious call was about to be dispatched.

When I heard that long *beeeeep,* I stopped what I was doing and listened. I never wanted the dispatcher to have to repeat the address.

I heard my unit number, and I knew that this alert—this emergency—was going to be my call. The dispatcher said, "2341 (me), 3-30 in progress, shots fired with injuries," and she gave the address of the Sayonara Bar. I was driving southbound on West

12th Avenue, approaching the bridge over a canal at 53rd Street and all types of crazy emotions began: fear, excitement, dread, and it was tough to focus on what the dispatcher was saying.

As the dispatcher continued speaking, I came over the top of that small bridge, and I could see the Sayonara through my windshield. I was that close, and in my rearview mirror, I could see the tiny pinprick of my backup's blue lights a mile away.

I didn't have the time or the need to use my own blue lights or siren because I was already pulling into the parking lot.

People were pouring out of the bar and into the parking lot—twenty or thirty of them—then the dispatcher added, "Subjects are still on the scene, armed with shotguns and machine guns—multiple victims down."

When adrenaline kicks in, fear leaves, and training takes over. Without being aware of drawing it, my gun was in my hand, and I was standing in front of this huge crowd of people who were yelling and screaming in Spanish and pointing inside the bar.

I stood behind the open door of my car and pointed my gun at them, thinking any one of them was about to kill me. There was no fear of death; all I felt was busy and sensory overload.

The parking lot was dark, but from where I was standing I could see several victims lying on the floor through the open door of the bar. I heard the siren from my backup officer's car getting closer, and someone in the crowd said in English the shooters had fled.

I moved toward the door, trying to keep my gun on the people in the parking lot and watch the door at the same time, all while wondering if I would hear the gunshot that would kill me. I thought later how foolish I was to enter the bar alone, but I knew people were dying inside, and it was my duty to try to save them.

I walked into the bar and saw one man was clearly dead. I knelt down next to another victim who was still breathing. He stared up at me, and I told him, "You're going to be okay." Bullet wounds are usually pretty obvious, but I found nothing. Then his eyes stopped tracking me and dilated, his ragged breathing stopped, and I could find no pulse.

I found out later this man had had his hands up, like he was surrendering, and a bullet had hit him in the armpit and exited the other side. Because he was lying on the floor with his hands at his sides, I couldn't see the wound. I imagine the bullet hit his heart, his lungs, his spine, or any combination of them.

I had my hand on his arm, and he was alive—then he wasn't. He was the first person to die on me.

Did he hear me? Did he even understand English? I still wonder today, but at the time, I just moved on to the next victim.

The parking lot and the inside of the bar were in organized chaos. Rescue trucks, fire engines, detectives, supervisors, and my fellow officers were all arriving. Orders were being given, victims were treated, inner and outer perimeters were designated. Four different radio frequencies and transmissions made communications challenging. Adding to the dozens of emergency vehicles in the parking lot, the media began arriving.

I was the officer assigned to write the report, and I had free access to the entire scene. There was a pool table in the back room, and what I found in there was pretty gruesome.

First, there was blood everywhere—on the walls, on the floor, and on the ceiling. Some of it was smeared, some of it was in big pools, some of it was simple drops, and some of it was sprayed out in unique patterns. The smell of blood was overpowering—metallic, coppery.

My boots slid on the bloody ceramic tile, and I was careful as

I walked toward the pool table. The green felt on the pool table was almost obscured with blood, and tiny gray balls rested all over its surface. Mixed in with these balls were pieces of what looked like the packaged ground beef in a grocery store, different shades of reds, pinks, and whites. Strings of this, like beef coming out of a grinder, hung from the ceiling and from the light fixture above the table.

The tiny gray balls were birdshot from a shotgun. I realized they were also on the floor and it was the birdshot I was slipping on.

Witnesses said a man with a sawed-off shotgun fired it into the pool room. Some of the witnesses said the shooter accidentally shot his own hand off when it slipped in front of the barrel, and others said the victim was an innocent man defending himself and someone had taken him to a local hospital.

Many of the people outside claimed they had been in the bathroom when the shooting occurred and saw nothing. If that's the case, that was one crowded bathroom, as it had only one stall.

***

This call, and in particular, that man's death, haunted me for months. It's easy now to think how bizarre I could make that moment sound: the act of dying, the spirit leaving, and knowing I was the last person he would ever see. I had stood over him; I had promised him he would be okay, then he died. But over time, the memory of his death blended in with others. In doing so, I was changing—I had been thrown into the fire, and I survived.

But today, that man's death affects me just as much as it did years ago. It's as if I've lost the tough veneer that sheltered me from the trauma of death, and now I'm exposed.

I never heard if any arrests were made in this case. In the 1980s, the Medellín Drug Cartel, dubbed the Colombian Cowboys for their violent elimination of competition, was at their peak, and scenes like this were playing out all over South Florida. In the next few weeks, both the Mariel Boatlift and the McDuffie Riots would begin, and things got much worse.

Chapter 9

The Pontiac

I had been on patrol for days and had not written a single traffic ticket. I wondered if my supervisors had noticed. I was a rookie, still on probation, and I didn't want to be thought of as lazy or unproductive. They probably could not have cared less, but it worried me, so I started looking for a traffic offender.

The next night, around two in the morning, a driver ran a red light right in front of me. I was exhilarated and nervous, which are not the best emotions when making serious decisions. I was about to write my first traffic ticket, or so I thought.

I activated my blue lights and rotating blue beams reflected all around me. I expected the car to pull off the road immediately as they had always done when I was in training—but the car took off in a cloud of dust.

"No!"

My vehicle, a Pontiac Bonneville with several hundred thousand miles on it, was one of the city's oldest and least desirable cars in the fleet. It steered and braked like an old boat. I hit the gas, and I was trying to decide what to say on the radio when the car ran through another red light, and I followed right behind. The red light was at the intersection of East 8th Avenue and Okeechobee Road, two of the busiest roads in Hialeah, and even at two in the morning there was traffic.

I had a brief awareness of headlights shining through my passenger door, then a tremendous impact.

I would not be writing any citations that night. In fact, I was lucky someone didn't write me one.

The car that hit me was a brand-new, black Chevrolet Z-28 Camaro.

I jumped out of my smoking car and ran over to the Camaro. Inside was a young Korean couple, and the woman was about six months pregnant. They were wearing hospital scrubs, nurses on their way to work at Jackson Memorial Hospital.

I had totaled their brand-new car, risked injuring them and their unborn child, yet they were worried they had hurt me and that the accident was somehow their fault.

I thanked God they were uninjured. I apologized repeatedly, and I waited for several days for my termination papers to make their way down the chain of command. What I got was a written reprimand and a day off without pay.

I had made one of the worst rookie mistakes possible—well, I guess it could have been worse. Still, I dodged a bullet that night, and it was a long time before I searched for traffic offenders again.

CHAPTER 10

RACISM

What can be a more delicate subject for a white police officer to deal with today than racism? It was just as sensitive in 1980, and one of the earliest events in my career was a race riot.

When I was very young, one of the first black persons I saw was the child who portrayed "Buckwheat," a character in the old TV show Our Gang. In those early years the only black people on TV I can remember played the parts of servants or slaves, as in Gone With The Wind, and it was common for white actors to wear blackface to portray black characters. This may sound incredible and racist now, but it was the truth then.

Hialeah in the mid and late fifties was an all-white town, and I cannot remember ever driving into the black sections of Miami. I'm sure we did, and I'm sure I saw blacks in Hialeah as a child, but it just wasn't significant. At that age, I didn't know anything about race; people were just people.

Not long after moving into a newer section of Hialeah, my family went to a cafeteria called St. Clairs after church one Sunday. I was seven or eight years old, and restaurants were new to us because eating out was a luxury we couldn't often afford.

After I walked through the buffet line, I watched the servers take my tray to our table. They had a foreign accent, and to me, they were elegant, as if they might have been royalty in another country. Unlike me, their skin was almost black, and it shone with a deep, bluish sheen.

Another day, as I walked through G.C. Murphy's store with my mother, I stopped at the water fountains and started to drink from one of them.

My mom said, "Not that one" and pointed to the sign attached to the front of it. Colored.

Years later, in my junior high history class, I learned about slavery and civil rights. There were no black students in my schools. It wasn't until my last year of senior high school that the first African American student enrolled at Hialeah High, but I never saw him because he was on a different class schedule.

Integration began after I graduated, and it wasn't until I worked at Ranch House that I had the chance to interact with African Americans.

In all my years on the Hialeah Police Department, I never saw an officer treat or speak to an African American any differently than a white or Hispanic person. If they were victims or witnesses, they were treated respectfully. If they were suspects, they were treated the same as any other white or Hispanic suspect was treated. Were any of my fellow officers racists? Possibly, but I never saw the signs.

But I did profile. Everyone has heard the term, and I'm sure most people immediately think—racism! But it wasn't, at least for me it wasn't. I stopped a lot of white people based on their skin color. I stopped them as they bought drugs in a black neighborhood.

***

The other day I pulled out my elementary school yearbook and looked through the pages at the names and the faces. There were no African Americans, and there were only a few Hispanics as well—maybe five percent. It wasn't until 1960, as the Cubans were fleeing Fidel Castro's dictatorship, that the demographics of South Florida began to change. I didn't even know what Hispanic meant, and Cuba could have been just another neighborhood. It would be years later when I started working for Ranch House that I made my first African American friend, a fellow busboy. But when I was seven years old, I didn't see the difference. My friends were my friends; I just thought they had a better tan than I did.

Chapter 11

The McDuffie Riots

In December of 1979, while I was still in the academy, Arthur McDuffie, an African American man, died after leading police officers on an eight-minute high-speed chase. It became newsworthy once it was discovered the man had not died from crash injuries, but from being beaten to death with flashlights. Four white Miami-Dade County officers were charged in his death.

The city of Hialeah shares a border with Miami and is part of Miami-Dade County. As the trial neared its end, every police department in South Florida was on high alert.

In May of 1980, an all-white jury found the officers not guilty, and the black communities of Liberty City (Miami-Dade County) and Overtown (Miami) erupted in violence known as the McDuffie Riots.

I had been on my own for two months when the McDuffie riots started on May 17, 1980, and lasted for four days.

On the afternoon of the 17th, the day the trial verdict was announced, I got a phone call telling me to report to work immediately. We didn't have take-home radios during my first few years so all I had to listen to was the FM radio in my car.

During that thirty-minute drive to the station, I listened to eyewitness accounts of victims being pulled from their cars and beaten to death, buildings burning, businesses being looted, and bodies lying dead in the streets.

I made it to the station around 4 p.m. and even the station was in chaos. All three shifts were now on duty, and officers were still being recalled from their days off. Most officers grabbed their gear and headed out to the affected areas.

Those officers were tasked with keeping the rioters from entering our city. Barricading the streets with their patrol cars, they allowed only residents of Hialeah and injured victims in. Hialeah has three major hospitals, and fire-rescue trucks and ambulances were all trying to make their way west out of the riot zone.

I was assigned to patrol a zone on the western edge of the city, away from all the chaos happening on the opposite side of the city, but I listened on the radio as my fellow officers dealt with the exodus of victims fleeing the riots.Those victims had no clue as to what was happening and were caught up in it on their drive home from work.

Most of the major roadways from downtown Miami ran right through the worst affected areas. The majority of these victims were motorists: men, women, and children who had been hit with bottles and bricks. Some had been pulled out of their cars and beaten. I could hear the desperation in the officers' voices as they were trying to route the flood of victims seeking aid and shelter. All our hospitals were overwhelmed in the first few hours.

Roughly ninety percent of our officers were assigned to assist and guard Hialeah's eastern border, and I was part of the other ten percent left to patrol the city. All night I listened to the madness as I patrolled my eerily quiet zone. Frustrated, I patrolled my assigned area, and as quiet and serene as my zone was, I had no doubt as to how bad things were elsewhere.

My zone was three miles from Hialeah's eastern border, currently called zone three. I pulled into the parking lot of the Hialeah Speedway and got out of my car. The entire eastern horizon glowed reddish-orange, like a sunrise. Trapped within this glow were four or five huge columns of black smoke rising thousands of feet into the night sky. The columns blotted out everything behind them and were then blown sideways where they formed into a single massive black cloud that covered all of South Florida. It looked like film footage of a war zone.

Hundreds of businesses were burning, including one of the largest tire dealerships in Florida. The burning rubber tires disintegrated into acrid soot that choked us and burned our eyes as it rained down all night.

Over the next sixteen hours, I went from one boring call to another that night and into the next morning. When they finally called us in, the officers who'd covered the riot zones described what they had seen and done on the perimeter. Like exhausted combat veterans, the officers' faces looked as if the hours and hours of running on adrenaline had taken its toll and they had nothing left in them.

What I heard from them was both gruesome and exciting, two very conflicting emotions.

***

The next night we all doubled up, two officers per car, and I was paired with a friend of mine, one of my academy classmates. We were told to join other officers on a perimeter check-point at NW 37th Avenue, our border with the county police.

Finally, I was going to be in the thick of it.

As we approached our assigned post, a dozen afternoon shift officers stood behind several patrol cars blockading the street. Behind them, the same dark, orange glow of fire and smoke blocked out the horizon.

Just as we stepped out of the patrol car, night turned to day as flashing gunfire exploded. I watched as those officers fired until their guns were empty, reloaded, and fired again.

The officers manning the perimeter had seen a driver fleeing from Metro Dade officers with his lights off, and at the last minute accelerated in an apparent attempt to ram the barricade.

The driver lost control of his car and smashed through the block wall of a junkyard, creating a huge hole. The driver jumped and escaped through the hole, leaving his female passenger in the car.

It took a few minutes to get her out as officers were still trying to find the driver inside the junkyard. The intoxicated woman's bloodcurdling screams seemed to go on forever.

"Please don't kill me, don't let them kill me!" she screamed, over and over.

The woman suffered only minor shrapnel wounds to her thigh, and we never found the driver, at least not then.

During the rest of that night and the next, several shots were fired at us from far down the street. They sounded like angry bees, and I heard them skipping off the asphalt as they came toward us. Most sounded as if they had lost their energy by the time they reached us, but it kept us alert. Other than the occasional ricochet, the glow and smell of the fires, the rest of the night was uneventful.

By the third night, the National Guard had been called in, and the rioting had begun to slow down. Most of the fires were out but the looting continued. I was sent back to the same perimeter post and joined about a half dozen Florida National Guardsmen.

I was the only police officer on this post, and one of the guardsmen said I was in charge. They could not load their weapons without my authorization. I thought that was pretty crazy; after all, I had only two months of experience. Pointing to all the shell casings lying around on the street from the night before, I said it was a good idea for them to load their weapons.

Later in the week, I saw the car that had crashed through the junkyard wall parked in the mayor's spot at city hall. I didn't count them, but I heard there were over a hundred bullet holes and every piece of glass was shot out.

Life slowly returned to normal in the next several weeks, but eighteen people were killed and over 350 were injured during those first few days.

There would be two lesser riots in the coming years, the Neville Johnson case in 1982 and the William Lozano case in 1989. These were reported as civil unrest by our politicians, not as riots, but trust me—buildings were looted and set on fire, people were beaten and curfews were established—they were riots.

Chapter 12

The Mariel Boatlift

The Mariel boatlift was a mass emigration of Cubans who traveled from Cuba's Mariel Harbor to Key West between April and October of 1980. Flotillas of private boats set sail from Key West with the expectation of bringing friends and loved ones to the United States.

When the private boats arrived in Cuba, they found that for every relative or friend, they were forced by Cuban soldiers to take ten strangers, most of them prisoners who had been released from the Cuban jails and mental health facilities by Fidel Castro. As many as 125, 000 Cubans reached Florida.

Crime became rampant. Our average homicide rate prior to 1980 was less than twenty but soon soared to over sixty during that first year. Other violent crimes increased as well and for years, officers were overwhelmed dealing with Marielitos or Balseros, as they were called.

I can still imagine Castro laughing at President Jimmy Carter as the boats vanished over the horizon.

CHAPTER 13

THE BULL

It was the summer of 1980, and I was on the midnight shift. It was the time of night when the heat had finally dissipated, but it was still so humid that dew covered my windshield and shimmered on the grass. It can get real spooky at four in the morning.

The streets were silent and deserted. The bakery trucks, milk trucks, and newspaper trucks wouldn't begin their deliveries for an hour or two. Even my radio had been silent for hours, and I played with the volume, afraid things were happening, but maybe I had accidentally turned the radio down or off. Just to make sure they weren't trying to dispatch me on a call, I kept turning up the volume knob.

I was in zone four, where I used to live, a mostly residential area, and on the midnight shift, it was one of the most boring areas of the city. I wished I was in another part of town patrolling the warehouses, looking for burglars or the crackheads walking the streets.

The alert tone sounded—and I had the volume up so loud it scared the shit out me. It was two quick beeps, not the long tone of an emergency. I heard my number and the memory of the Sayonara Bar hit me. For a brief moment, I feared my wish had come true.

The signal was a 14, conduct an investigation. Someone had reported a bull in a residential area. There were no ranches for miles and miles, no pastures, no stables, no farms—nothing. Not just a cow, though—a bull.

So I wrote down the call and listened to the clicking mics and the snickering on the radio from my fellow officers. They all thought the call was bullsh*t.

As I headed toward the call, I recognized the address, a corner house on a residential intersection of West 12th Avenue and 60th Street; it was Dr. Markarian's office. I knew the house because I used to live right down the street, and my mother was his patient.

In daylight, the house always looked odd; unlike all the other houses, there was never any grass in the front yard. This yard was all white gravel with several white marble or concrete statues, and a pair of working water fountains. At night, it looked like a cemetery.

I stepped out of the car, and other than the sound of my car's engine, it was silent. I surmised the term "dead of night" actually referred to the dead because this was when ghosts would be have been out and about. Wisps of humidity floated through the beam of my headlights, and the misty fog absorbed noise the way snow does.

About thirty feet away, standing among the eclectic collections of sculptures and fountains, was a white Brahman bull, which must have weighed two thousand pounds. Although I'd never seen a Brahman bull, the big hump on its back told me this was indeed a Brahman bull.

The bull stood motionless, looking at me just like cows look at you when you get near their fence. It was the perfect final piece in Dr. Markarian's collection of yard art.

I returned to my car to tell the dispatcher there was a bull at the address, and for a moment there was silence on the radio. Then a few of my zone partners said they were on the way to help.

Meanwhile, the bull started to move, lumbering toward Sparks Park, which was right across the street, and I had no clue as to what I was supposed to do. Do I try to stop it? And just how was I going to do that?

Another police car glided up silently, headlights off, cutting through the mist like a ship cuts through the sea, and the two of us watched the big bull cross West 12th Avenue, one of the main roads, and thankfully, there was still no traffic.

Other officers began to arrive and we decided to form a line of cars, bumper to bumper, and followed the bull as it strolled along the park's fence. As the bull reached the park's office it turned into the parking lot, and there were enough police cars now to corral it inside. I'd never seen bulls jump over cars or try to push them out of their way, but I assumed it was possible.

Most of us stepped out of our cars and watched, but stayed close by so we could jump back in if the bull came after us.

Someone in communications remembered there was a rodeo several miles west of the city, and they sent an officer to ask if the bull was theirs. It was and while we waited, the morning traffic started moving, and the drivers were all gawking at this huge white bull surrounded by patrol cars in the park. Fortunately, a truck with a cattle trailer pulled up, and two sleepy cowboys loaded the bull into their trailer.

The bull had walked three or four miles through a residential neighborhood before the first person called it in. I can picture some poor guy with insomnia looking out the window of his bedroom as the huge white bull strolled through his yard.

CHAPTER 14

THE DENTIST

There is no specific amount of time when an officer knows they've passed from being a rookie to an experienced officer. Some say one year, but I felt the transition within the first three months on the road.

While I was a trainee in the police academy, a homicide instructor told us we, as police officers, were in the top ten professions to commit suicide. I was surprised to hear dentists were number one.

In 2015, *Mental Health Daily* reported dentists dropped to number two and police officers were ranked number three. Why would a dentist want to kill himself?

Not long after I was released to work on my own, I was dispatched to one of my first suicides—a dentist.

It was after midnight, and the call was to a small shopping complex. I pulled up next to the only two cars in the lot and saw the lights on inside the office. A woman met me at the door. She was either the cleaning woman or someone a family member had asked to check on the man or maybe both.

She led me to an exam room where the victim, who appeared to be in his middle thirties, was lying in a fully reclined dentist chair, and except for the IV in his arm, he looked like he was sleeping. He was cold to the touch, and I guessed he had been dead for several hours.

I asked communications to notify a detective, and I waited until one arrived. I wrote my quick report: *Arrived to find victim deceased and notified the detective bureau. No other information,* and I left.

Was it an accidental overdose or was he addicted to pain medication? Later in the week, I saw the detective and asked him about the man. It was a suicide, and he had left a note explaining his reasons for ending his life. I never learned what was in the empty IV bag.

I often think of the dead as I stand in the room with them. What type of person were they? If they were the victim of suicide, I wondered then and still do, what drove them to end their lives? I have my own share of depression at times, and if I'm not careful, I find myself grieving for them.

CHAPTER 15

HALLOWEEN

We don't hear much about suicide by hanging in the news; in fact, suicides are rarely mentioned at all unless the deceased is a celebrity.

On October 31, 1980, I was just leaving the station about 10:30 at night when the dispatcher hit the alert tone and sent me as a backup officer to assist with a call about a man hanging from a tree.

It was Halloween and most people, like myself, feel different on this night. Maybe it's the memory of wearing costumes and trying to scare each other as kids, or we think of movies like *Friday the 13th* or *Aliens* or *A Nightmare on Elm Street*. Those memories are imprinted on us whether we know it or not. So I thought because it was Halloween this was just someone's idea of a prank—but it wasn't.

It was a corner house, and as I got out of my car, another officer and his partner pulled up at the same time. The partner, a reserve officer, was an older man who volunteered once or twice a month. The three of us looked through the chain-link fence into the backyard, where the man hung lifeless from a rope tied to a tree branch.

The other officers got to him first and thought he was still alive. The reserve officer stood under the victim, ready to catch him, as the first officer sliced through the rope with his knife. As the blade cut through the last strands, the body fell on the older man and pinned him to the ground.

The reserve officer didn't scream, but silently, his arms and legs flailed around in a panic. The victim was a big, heavy man, and the impact probably knocked the wind out of the officer. I rolled the victim's body off the still-silent but terrified officer.

He never rode with us again.

I wish I knew more about this victim and why he decided to end his life, but this wasn't my call. The other officer stayed and wrote the report.

This was the first hanging I saw, but it was not the last. I had no time to really think much about it that night as it was Halloween, and Halloween in Hialeah was one of the busiest nights of the year.

CHAPTER 16

THE MODEL IN THE CADILLAC

It was a Saturday, and I had just started my shift at the busy commercial area of Westland Mall when I was dispatched to a routine traffic accident. The accident was in front of one of the big entrances to the mall, and the traffic was heavy. I had to weave in and out of three lanes of traffic using my lights and siren to get to it.

A big beige Cadillac had been broadsided in the passenger doors by an equally big car. The Cadillac was hit so hard it had been pushed sideways off the road and into the landscaping at the mall entrance.

I parked at an angle behind the first car, still in the street, which forced traffic into the open lanes and protected all of us as I prepared to start a report. The front end of this car was totaled, steam was coming out from under the crushed hood, and hot water was pouring out of the radiator. The driver was an older woman who was still sitting inside the car, shaken up, but otherwise okay.

From thirty feet away I could see the driver of the Cadillac was slumped over the steering wheel, and I told the dispatcher I needed fire-rescue as I ran over and opened the door.

The driver was a young woman. She was unconscious, her head rested on the steering wheel, and her blond hair hung forward like a curtain, obscuring her face. She was still strapped in with her seat belt. I couldn't see any signs of injury, but she was gasping for air, more of an unconscious spasm than a breath. I'd seen this before, and I knew it was not good.

Fearing she would suffocate, I supported her head and neck and eased her back into the seat, hoping it would help her breathe, but the reflexive gasping continued. Her exhale with each spasm was awful. Her chest was rising as it filled with air, so I knew she was getting oxygen. She had a pulse, too, but I couldn't think of anything else to do so I just knelt next to her and watched…helplessly.

While waiting for the fire-rescue truck, I took a good look at her. Again, there were no signs of injury, no blood, no broken bones, no swelling, or any other trauma I would expect to see in an unconscious victim.

I guessed she was about twenty, thin and athletic, wearing shorts—and it was difficult to look at her face. She was probably an attractive woman, but the grimace on her face each time she gasped was horrific, like she was wearing a mask of pain.

Rescue finally arrived, and they put her on a backboard and took her away. I could tell by their urgency and the look on their faces they were worried, too.

It took me about forty-five minutes to get everything I needed for the report and to tow the two cars away, then I headed to Palmetto General Hospital.

The woman died before I got there; her body was in one of the curtained ER rooms, but I didn't want or need to see her.

I notified the dispatcher of her death and an AIU (accident investigation unit) officer was assigned to follow up with a traffic homicide report, which would be much more detailed than mine.

I'd been to this hospital so many times already most of the nurses knew my name. They told me several of the woman's organs had been ripped free from the impact, and she'd bled out internally.

Although a seat belt can keep someone from being ejected or keep their head from hitting the steering wheel or windshield, it can't keep the liver or spleen from slamming into their ribcage on impact.

The next day I saw the accident investigator at the station. He said he had to make the death notification to the woman's family, and it was a tough one.

"She was a successful model," he said.

She had appeared uninjured in her seat—picture perfect, I thought—except for her face. I had seen so many people in much worse shape survive, and that bothered me.

I saw her photo on her driver's license later, but somehow today, I can't recall what she looked like.

All I can see is that mask of pain.

During my part of the investigation, there were no witnesses to interview and the surviving driver told me that she had the right of way with a green light when the Cadillac turned left in front of her. Once I learned the victim had died, I left the ensuing investigation up to the AIU officer, and I don't know if either driver was found at fault.

Chapter 17

The Hot Walker

After two years in road patrol, I was reassigned to a tactical unit called 1A. We wore plain clothes, we drove old cars, and our job was to look for in-progress calls to catch criminals in the act.

One night several officers in my unit and I were dispatched to a shooting at the Hialeah Race Track stables. The Hialeah Race Track, once a beautiful art deco horse track known for its pink flamingos, was in decline by 1981, as was horse racing throughout South Florida.

I stood at the entrance to the stables. There were several dozen of them and each one held up to twenty horses. Some were awake and watching us. There were an equal number of dormitories, all built in the late 30s, which were a combination of concrete block and wood. Tall ficus trees surrounded each row of buildings and partially obscured my view of the grandstands.

The dormitories housed the low-level workers employed by the horse's owners. These workers had different titles: hot walkers, who walked the horses to cool them down after a workout; and grooms, who cared for the horses and cleaned the stables, etc. Like carnival workers, they traveled with a certain owner or a certain horse from track to track all over the country.

I found the victim on a sidewalk outside one of the stables.

The victim, a hot walker, had been shot in the face but was still alive. Several of us knelt down to help him, but there wasn't much we could do except ensure he didn't choke to death on his own blood.

He tried to tell us what happened and who shot him, but the bullet had destroyed his tongue and jaw, and the severe wounds made it hard to understand him. Rescue arrived soon after and began prepping him for transport, but he died not long after arriving at the hospital.

We were pretty sure we understood the name of the gunman, and some of the victim's coworkers recognized the name. They said the victim and the other man had argued earlier and gave us the man's description. The suspect was employed by a different owner but housed in the same dorm. He had fled from the track but was arrested nearby a few days later.

The victim was about twenty years old and from a wealthy family in either New York or Canada. He had left home and joined the horse racing community as an opportunity to see the world.

The state's attorney was reluctant to take the case to trial; there were no witnesses and no evidence other than the dying man's declaration, which was, truthfully, hard to understand. But the victim's family was persistent, and eventually I found myself in the witness chair along with several of my fellow officers and paramedics.

The verdict was not guilty. I know the system is meant to protect the innocent, but I also know a guilty man walked free that day. It was a weak case, but the pain and disappointment lingered for weeks.

***

This homicide occurred sometime in 1981—thirty-eight years later I can still see the kid's face as he was trying to speak to me. I see the victim's family in the courtroom, the look in their eyes, hoping I was going to say something that would bring justice for their son and brother. I relive those vivid details when something triggers the memory, like watching the Kentucky Derby, then file them away.

CHAPTER 18

THE YAWN OF DEATH

While writing "The Model in the Cadillac," I recalled another similar death.

Just after dark one evening, I was dispatched to an 18, a hit-and-run traffic accident, this one involving a pedestrian, which was an all-too-frequent call.

When I arrived, a man in his late fifties was sitting up in the middle of the street. He was alone, in the dark, and about one hundred feet from the nearest streetlight. His shoes were about twenty feet away, placed perfectly next to each other as if he were still standing in them. He was drunk, and I recognized him as a man I'd arrested several times before.

He joked with me and with the paramedics when they arrived. All I could see were minor injuries— some road rash, a few cuts and scrapes, but the paramedics transported him to the hospital anyway. I remember one of their criteria for transporting him, even with such superficial injuries, was because the impact had knocked him out of his shoes.

I got to the hospital just a few minutes later where I saw him lying unconscious on an exam table. He was doing precisely what the woman in the Cadillac had done, gasping for breath, but because he was lying flat on his back it looked like an exaggerated yawn and a gasp at the same time. This gasping happened about every fifteen seconds, and his mouth opened so wide I expected to hear tendons snap or his jaw break.

The nurse told me they were prepping him for a CT scan, and they had listed him in critical condition. He died about four hours later, and I never learned what the cause of death was.

The man was never a bad drunk, more of a nuisance to his neighbors, and he never gave me a hard time. I've forgotten his jokes, or even if they were funny, but I hope he was drunk enough that he felt no pain during those last few hours of his life.

Chapter 19

The AIDS Epidemic

The AIDS epidemic and the homophobia following actor Rock Hudson's horrific death in 1985 from the disease was a great concern for first responders. At first, it was called the Gay Disease or the Gay Cancer. People refused to eat food cooked or served by a gay waiter and openly gay entertainers couldn't find work. People wouldn't shake hands with a gay man or even want to be in the same room. I can't imagine what the gay community was going through during those early years.

But it wasn't long before HIV was identified as the cause, blood and certain body fluids were how the virus was transmitted, and we learned anyone was capable of being infected. There was one newsworthy report of a straight housewife having been infected with HIV and later developed AIDS from her husband, a heroin addict.

Now it was not just gay men we feared, but blood and body fluids. There was also the fear that even someone's sweat could transmit the disease, or even a sneeze, and the sight of a used syringe could clear a room. I remember the panic I felt when I found one on a prisoner. The paranoia lasted for years.

Before this, coming in contact with someone else's blood was just part of the job. I probably had someone else's blood on me every single day. Now, touching someone else's blood was feared like the Black Death must have been feared in the 1300s.

I started carrying a box of latex surgical gloves in my car and kept a pair in my pocket all the time, but for the most part, they were useless. They took time to put on, time I never had when I needed them. I couldn't put them on while driving, and I couldn't call a time-out on the scene of an arrest. When I was fortunate to have them on, I often found them ripped and useless after handling a prisoner.

I tried wearing a thicker, tactical glove, but it was difficult to get my finger on the gun's trigger while wearing them. Some officers wore the fingerless gloves or cut the trigger finger part off, but what's the point then?

More than a few officers I worked with were exposed to HIV. Infected prostitutes or IV drug users would spit on officers or purposely bleed on them. One man was charged with attempted murder when he spit on an officer in our jail, but those charges were eventually dropped. That officer had to endure months of treatments to combat the possibility of infection. All this history of AIDS is meant to explain why this next simple car crash stands out in my mind.

One afternoon I was dispatched to a traffic accident, and on arrival, I saw the usual smashed-up cars and injured occupants. In Hialeah, we were fortunate to have fire-rescue paramedics respond within minutes, but on this day, I was alone.

I approached one of the cars and saw the driver behind the wheel had some pretty significant facial lacerations. Seat belts weren't used much then, and most cars didn't have airbags yet, and this kid's face had hit the windshield. Facial wounds bleed a lot, and he was covered in his own blood. As I leaned in through the window, the first thing he said was, "I'm HIV positive."

This was an ordinary-looking kid, probably late teens or early twenties, well dressed, healthy-looking, and I thought if he could be infected, everyone I met could be infected. Later I realized it must have taken great courage for him to tell me, and to this day, I thank him.

As he sat bleeding in his seat, I gave him a clean towel I kept in my car and told him to keep the pressure on the cuts on his face until paramedics arrived. I hope the kid lived, but the medicines hadn't yet been developed to stop the virus.

AIDS changed everything for first responders.

***

I thought I was finished with this chapter six months ago. It seemed perfect and expressed all I intended it to. Then I watched the movie *Philadelphia*—and I knew I wasn't finished.

The movie is set in the mid-1980s, and Tom Hanks' character had been fired when his coworkers learned he had AIDS. He found a homophobic attorney named Joe Miller, played by Denzel Washington, and the two of them sue his former bosses for discrimination.

The movie is rife with the paranoia of AIDS, and the fear and disgust directed toward homosexuals. That's the way it was in the 1980s—and I was that homophobic attorney, and I was his coworkers, and I was also a lot of the other characters.

I'm not sure if homophobia accurately describes the way we grew up thinking of gays. Phobia means fear, but the dictionary also uses the words *mistrust* and *discrimination,* which, to me, are more accurate terms to describe my attitude at the time.

When I was a kid, around the age of ten was when boys started noticing that other boys were different—those boys who didn't want to play football or play with frogs—we called them "sissies." We didn't know what sex was at the age of ten. But as we went through adolescence, we started calling them fags and homos.

I never physically bullied any of them or even called any of them by those names, but I listened to gay jokes, and I often told a few of my own. I look back now, and I suspect it was a way of showing that we, or I, wasn't gay, and it seemed important to me that my friends knew it. It's like gorillas pounding their chests I guess, some display of machismo.

When our kids were young, Susan watched *America's Top Model* and a few similar shows. I would often point out how gay some of the judges were, and I would make crude comments about them.

Then my sixteen-year-old son told me he was gay.

How many times during those years had I hurt him while he battled with his sexuality and his fear of telling us?

He asked me once, "Dad, do you think I would have chosen to live this way?"

I've had long talks with him since then, and I've apologized the best way I know how and he says we're okay. But I know if I've ever failed at being a parent, it was in hurting him with my homophobia.

I'm no longer a homophobe—my son, at the age of sixteen, taught me to be a better man.

Chapter 20

The Horse

Many of my memories are tragic. As I write them and when I read them later, I find myself in a dark place. When I'm done, those feelings, those depressing memories, linger for hours and sometimes days, like a migraine that just won't go away.

Some memories begin with tragedy, but end with a feeling of a job well done. After those calls were completed, I felt lighter on my feet; I had a little more spring in my step. This is one of those memories.

The Palmetto Expressway, a four-lane highway with a grassy swale in the 1980s and now eight lanes of solid concrete, runs north and south as it passes through Hialeah. We were often called to assist the Florida Highway Patrol with accidents that occurred on their roadway. One weekend I was dispatched to the Palmetto to help with an accident involving a horse.

As I pulled up, a crumpled car, a red Hialeah fire-rescue truck, and a brown horse were on the side of the road, half on the grassy swale and half in the emergency lane. I turned on my emergency lights and parked my car behind the horse to block the lane. As I walked over to the motionless horse, one of the firemen said they were taking the driver of the crumpled car to the hospital, and they left me alone with the injured horse.

I took a good look at the horse. She was a solid brown mare, a chestnut, and she was lying on her left side. A deep gash about eight inches long stretched across her right flank, and a river of dark blood ran down a concrete drainage ditch where it collected into a coagulated red pool six feet away.

The horse was breathing, and her big brown eye followed me as I moved around her, but she never raised her head. Fortunately for both of us, she never showed any signs of pain. I knelt down several times and talked to her, rubbed her neck and the white blaze between her eyes, and I hoped it calmed her some.

I asked the dispatcher to check on FHP's response and was told they were busy and there was no ETA. Meanwhile, passing motorists whizzed by a few feet away at seventy miles per hour. A few of them stopped or slowed down to gawk at the horse and some even asked if they could help. Some asked me why I hadn't shot it yet.

"Put it out of its misery!" more than a few people yelled. I know that most of them just wanted to see the gore.

I asked the dispatcher to look through the phone book for an emergency veterinarian; they found one, and I was told the ETA would be at least an hour.

While the horse and I waited, I listened to more motorists demand I shoot it, and several times, the thought crossed my mind. Eventually, the same fire-rescue team returned from the hospital, and I told them a vet was on the way. Seeing the amount of blood the horse had lost, they tried an IV to pump some plasma into her, but their needles were too short.

While we all waited on the side of the road, one of the paramedics told me he had talked to the car's driver. The driver said as he approached the horse and rider, someone had honked their horn, which startled the horse, and it turned into his lane. The driver said the man on the horse had just rented it for the day and didn't care about its injuries. The rider had only minor injuries, and a passing motorist picked him up and drove him away.

The fire-rescue team received another call and had to leave, and again I was alone with the horse, which continued to bleed, the pool of blood growing larger by the minute. She was still breathing comfortably but hadn't moved a muscle, and we, the mare and I, talked some more.

An hour later, a pick-up truck, a veterinarian sign on its door, towing a horse trailer pulled up next to me. I told the vet what I knew, and he looked at the pool of blood and shook his head.

"She can lose twice that amount of blood and it wouldn't kill her."

He fixed up an IV bag similar to fire-rescue's, but with a huge needle, and jammed it into one of her veins. He squeezed the bag dry, then another, and the horse stood up as if nothing had happened.

The vet loaded her into the trailer and said he would stitch her up when he got back and bill the owners if he could find them—then he left.

FHP never arrived, and I ended up writing the report. For the first and last time in my career, I used the little horse symbol on my traffic accident template. I waited for the wrecker to arrive and hook up the damaged car, then I left. I never heard from the rider, the horse's owner, or the veterinarian. NOI, no other information, as officers like to say.

***

I like animals.

A few years ago, a magnificent eight-point buck, with one of its front legs missing, struggled into my backyard. Even though it was nighttime, I could see it was dying. What was left of its leg was black with gangrene, and the buck was so weak it collapsed in my yard. I shot him with a .243, and I felt sick to my stomach and relieved at the same time. Knowing I had done the right thing didn't make it any easier.

In the morning I got a better look at the deer. It looked as if it had been hit by a car a week or so earlier and had been suffering ever since. Using my four-wheeler, I dragged it off the lawn and into the woods. I remembered that beautiful chestnut mare when I thought of this buck.

Chapter 21

Back to the Academy

At the end of 1983, our training lieutenant asked if I was interested in becoming a training advisor at the Metro-Dade Criminal Justice Building, the Academy.

"Do you think I have enough experience to teach?" I said. "I've only been on the road four years."

"Yes, I do! Everyone I've talked to says you're the officer I need."

"Lieutenant, I love working the road."

"So do I," he said. "But you won't regret the experience."

I thought about it that night. The offer was just too great to pass up. I remembered how much I admired my training advisors and the positive impact they had on me as a raw recruit.

I walked into his office the next day. "Sure, I'll take the job."

I taught three basic law enforcement classes during the next two years, and each class lasted five months. I took raw recruits with little or no experience in law enforcement, taught them the basics, and prepared them for their first day on patrol. I would love to go into great detail of how rewarding the experience was, but that is not why I'm writing this memoir, so I won't.

As a training advisor, I finally learned why cadets had to learn to march, why they spent hours and hours each week on the drill field, why they needed to salute the flag, why they had to stand at attention for long periods of time, and why the uniforms had to be so crisp.

It was all to prepare us for the powerful, graceful, and dignified show of respect as we honored our dead brothers and sisters in blue at their funerals.

***

Donald Kramer

As a training advisor in the academy, I attended many funerals of officers killed in the line of duty, usually with a few of my trainees and sometimes an entire class. One of those funerals was for a Miami Beach officer, Donald Kramer, shot and killed by a homeless man on February 25, 1984. My entire class of BLE 81 attended. We stood at attention, we saluted, and we marched in the formations we learned in the academy. I will never forget the moment, and I know those trainees will remember it also.

John Koppin

On December 26, 1984, less than a year after Donald Kramer's death, one of the trainees who marched during Officer Kramer's funeral, John Koppin, would die from an accidental gunshot wound while cleaning his firearm. He was my first class's guidon. A guidon is the narrow, pointed pennant, or the man carrying the pennant, in marching formations or into battle.

David Herring

David Herring, one of my trainees from BLE 86, died in September of 1986 from carbon monoxide poisoning while sitting in his patrol car. Patrol officers spend hours and hours sitting in our cars writing our reports while the engine is running, and in south Florida it's hot even at three in the morning, so the air conditioner is always running. David's car that night had a leak in the exhaust, and it filled the interior with carbon monoxide.

David was an easy-going, all-around great guy. I ran into him once soon after he graduated and remembered how excited he was to be out on the street enforcing the law. He died one month later.

Scott Rakow

Scott Rakow, another one of my trainees, would die in June 1988, shot while pursuing a drug suspect. The suspect was running away and fired over his shoulder with a .25-caliber automatic pistol and hit Scott in the forehead—an impossibly lucky shot. Scott was one of the sharpest cadets in the class, always in the top two or three in academics and fitness. If Scotty could be killed so easily, I knew I wasn't as invulnerable as I thought.

Bill Williams

William Williams was in my class, a fellow cadet in BLE 42; he would die on July 3rd, 2000.

Bill was a motorcycle officer with the city of Miami. He was working a funeral procession when one of the drivers in the procession decided they had gone far enough and made a left turn. Bill, moving from the last intersection to the head of the procession, collided with that car. He lived for a few days without regaining consciousness, then died. I saw most of my class at his funeral; some of them I had not seen in twenty years.

Each officer's death resulted in a blood drive, and Bill's was no exception. We lined up for Bill the same way we lined up for so many others. It was a helpless feeling, knowing a friend was dying, and giving blood was often all we could do.

The bloodmobile was an old bus, painted white with a big red heart on it. It was parked behind Jackson Memorial Hospital while Bill was still in ICU. I was in a long line of people waiting to donate. I recognized some of them, fellow officers and civilian employees, but I suspect most were just citizens hoping, like us, that Bill would live.

Even as I watched my own blood fill the bag, I doubted Bill would live. I had heard how seriously he was injured, and I knew the odds. But I did what I could do and hoped for the best.

There was motorcycle officer on our department who had a similar accident, and the odds were against him too. Jorge was in a coma for weeks, or maybe even months, but he survived. He had to relearn how to speak and how to walk and came back to work years later, a different person and was still working when I retired.

In November of 1986 as BLE 92 graduated, I found I missed working the streets. I asked for and was granted a transfer back to patrol where I took on the added role of a field training officer. I remembered what I liked about my two FTOs, and I tried to emulate their good qualities with my trainees.

Being an FTO was no piece of cake. Not only did I have to

keep myself alive, but the lives of my trainees were in my hands as well. It sounds melodramatic, I know, but at two in the morning, when it was only me and a kid who just graduated checking a burglar alarm, and we found a sledgehammer and big hole in the wall or a smashed-in front door, it could be pretty stressful.

CHAPTER 22

SUSAN

One summer day in 1984, I was in the parking lot of our station watching the Blue Angels practice for an air show when a little Honda Civic parked next to me. A tall, beautiful woman with long blonde hair stepped out. She was wearing the light blue shirt of a civilian employee, and as she headed for the communications building I said, " Hello," which was bold for me. I had always been a little slow when it came to meeting women.

She turned and smiled. She didn't say anything then, but ten years later I married her.

That was twenty-three years ago next week, as I write this.

Susan is my wife. She is also my confidante, the keeper of my secrets, the one I turn to when I'm depressed or angry. I know that's what spouses are supposed to do, but I feel Susan has gone above and beyond that call of duty; she is what keeps me grounded, and she transports me back from places I don't want to be. This may sound overly dramatic, but it's the truth.

Susan has her own share of painful memories. One I remember all too well was when a woman called 911 worrying that her son might have been in a car accident and asking if he was okay. Susan knew that the woman's son, a young high school student, had been killed in a horrific crash right outside his school. Her training prevented her from telling this poor mother the truth, something I know still bothers her today.

When I remember Susan telling me this, I see her pain, and I feel it too. Few people will experience this type of pain; it's a bond we share, not one that we've asked for, but one we live with just the same.

Just the other day, Susan and I were driving northbound on a highway, and she was telling me about a conversation she had with a friend earlier, something about trying a new church. What she was saying was running in the background of my brain, but I didn't really hear her. Instead, I was watching the southbound cars, and my mind was focused fifteen years in the past, remembering an old guy who had a seizure while driving.

Witnesses said they saw the grimace on the man's face as he was locked in the seizure. His foot accidentally mashed the accelerator of his big van as his elderly wife tried to steer from the passenger seat. The van crossed the center line and hit another car head-on, killing everyone in both vehicles.

I had been on my way into work that day and saw the aftermath—the debris field from the wreck was almost a block long.

That's what I was seeing and feeling when I realized Susan had asked me a question.

"What?"

"Where were you just now?"

I lied and said I was thinking about a chapter in my new novel. I figured she didn't need to know what I was really thinking, at least not then.

She is also a great editor and is the first reader of everything I write so eventually she will read this, too.

Not only do I love her, I think of her as my anchor to the real world, to my sanity, and I try to tell her that as often as I can.

CHAPTER 23

EMILIO MIYARES

"Good men must die, but death cannot kill their names."

—Proverbs

So begins the second half of my career as a patrol officer.

In November of 1986, I had just transferred from training back to road patrol and was working the afternoon shift when my friend and fellow officer Emilio Miyares was shot and killed. He wasn't the first officer I worked with over the years who died tragically, but none affected me more profoundly.

Emilio and I were hired by the department at about the same time, he as a complaint officer and I as a police officer. As a junior officer on midnights, I was often called into the communications building to relieve the desk sergeant for his meal break. Sometimes that sergeant would take the day off, and I would spend my entire shift on the desk. It was during those times that I met Emilio, and we remained good friends for the next six years.

Emilio had a rare gift of connecting with others, an infectious smile, and a personality to match. Talking with him, even for a moment, made me feel somehow lighter, and I walked away a little happier than I was before—I felt refreshed and rejuvenated.

Emilio didn't stay in communications long. He soon became a sworn police officer working road patrol and eventually he transferred to the traffic unit as a motorman. He was living his dream and always had a big smile as he rode his Kawasaki out of the station every day.

November 6th was my day off, and a group of us from the department had planned to get together later at the Crown Rocking Lounge for drinks, but that afternoon the phone rang, and it was Susan, my future wife, telling me Emilio had been shot.

My gut reaction was I had misheard what she said. Then it hit me like a sledgehammer.

Emilio has been shot! I thought, maybe, it was just a minor flesh wound.

"Is he okay?"

"No." There was a long pause. "He didn't make it." She choked up, and in a whisper she said, "The guys on the road don't know it yet—they're still searching for the shooter."

The administration didn't want the officers to know Emilio had died; they were afraid the officers would execute the man out of rage.

I drove to the station that afternoon, but the rest of the day is just a blur.

Emilio and his partner were patrolling on their motorcycles, doing what motormen do, when they heard a suspicious persons call on the radio. *Two men on a bus bench, possibly involved in an armed robbery.* Normally patrol officers, like me, handle calls like that, but none were available.

Emilio and the other officer found the two men behind the shopping mall. The men took off running in different directions, leaving a machine gun behind, and the two officers split up to chase the suspects. Emilio caught and confronted one of them inside the mall.

One witness said Emilio had his gun drawn but hesitated. "You could see it in his face—he didn't want to shoot the guy."

Another account said Emilio struggled with the guy, and he took the gun out of Emilio's holster.

Yet another witness said, "When I went home last night, all I could see was the cop on his knees with his hands up, screaming, 'Wait, wait!' I saw it again and again."

Either way, the man fired four shots at point-blank range, hitting Emilio three times in the chest.

South Florida is hot, and most motormen don't wear a bulletproof vest. Emilio didn't stand a chance.

There was a manhunt, and several hours later Samuel Rivera was found hiding behind a house and arrested. His brother Alberto was arrested the next day.

Emilio was killed in zone three, the zone I worked every day, and it happened on my day off. Had I been working, maybe I would have gotten the call. It's a haunting thing, like some of the other scenes I describe in this collection of memories. I wonder if I had been on duty, could I have helped Emilio, would I have been the officer dispatched to the call, would I have been killed, or would my vest have saved me?

Many hours later, most of the group got together at the Crown Rocking Lounge and raised a few too many shot glasses of tequila, blue blazers, root beer shooters, and who knows what else to Emilio's memory.

There was a huge funeral at All Angels Episcopal Church, the church Emilio and his family attended every Sunday. Thousands of officers from all over Florida and many other states attended. There were hundreds of police motorcycle escorts, honor guards, politicians, TV trucks, police helicopter flyovers, media helicopters, police horses, cadets, and even schoolchildren. It was a lot to take in.

The hardest parts of the funeral were watching them bring the casket out, seeing Emilio's new widow, trying to hold a salute as the hearse approached, and hearing the sounds of my friends sobbing as it passed.

There was a feeling of disbelief that lasted for weeks; after all, we thought we were invulnerable, and God was on our side. I don't understand why I felt those two feelings, after all, I had been to several police funerals already, but even after Emilio's death, that feeling of immortality remained.

Every year the anniversary of Emilio's death is marked on the Hialeah Police Facebook page, and we relive a little bit of the grief we felt then, we reflect on his life and our own, and we remember the joy he brought into our lives.

Emilio has been gone now longer than he was alive. He had the opportunity to live his dream, to do good, and it cost him his life. It cost his wife her husband, and his kids their father.

Samuel Rivera died in prison in 1994.

Emilio was, and will always be, 27 years old.

Chapter 24

Pete Cainas

Pete's death was another one that hit me hard. I had worked with Pete for years, on the same shift and often in the same squad.

While working as a patrol officer, Pete was also attending law school at the University of Miami. Not long after he graduated, he quit the department and went to work for the state attorney's office. I would see him now and then in court handling DUI and misdemeanor cases. He confided in me it wasn't what he had expected and missed being on the road. A year or so later, he resigned from the SAO. He was rehired by Hialeah, and once again we worked the afternoon shift together.

Not long after he returned, I read one of his reports, something mundane, but he had written it like a law brief—the crazy legalese, almost-cryptic narrative used by attorneys so no one can understand what it really says.

One of us came up with the idea of opening the dictionary and picking an odd word at random and trying to fit it into one of our reports each night. My word one night was *concubine,* or as described in the dictionary, a mistress. Another definition is a woman who lives with a man but has a lower status than his wife or wives.

Lucky for me, one of my first calls that night was a domestic; the complainant wanted to report threats against her by her lover's wife.

Several days later I was called into the deputy chief's office. The woman had read the report and was not happy being referred to as a concubine. The deputy chief was also not happy.

While we were fooling with obscure words for our reports, South Florida was suffering a severe drought and instituted water restrictions. This wasn't the first water crisis but now the police officers were tasked with enforcing it. We were issued a small citation book, and if we were dispatched on a water call, we were ordered to write a report and issue a citation. This was a major frustration for us.

We had bigger problems—criminals were targeting tourists driving rental cars as they exited Miami International Airport. The tourists were dragged from their cars, beaten and robbed, and it was happening every day. The rental companies used specific license plates beginning with a "Z" and expiring in June, so it was easy for the thugs to spot them.

Tourists were also easy targets because they knew nothing about the area and were distracted by their new surroundings. And most important to the criminals, tourists would seldom return for a trial if an arrest was made. It came to a head when a woman from Germany was killed while fighting off a purse snatcher. The rash of robberies, and now this woman's death, became international news.

As officers, we wanted to concentrate all of our free time patrolling the main road out of the airport, and these petty water violations were eating into our valuable patrol time. While people were being beaten, robbed, and now shot and killed, we were handing out meaningless citations.

I got one of those water violation calls around 10 p.m. one night and wrote my obligatory report, which began, "It was a warm, dry evening as I closed the distance between me and the scene of the crime." I thought I would never see the report again, and I wrote it not to be humorous but out of frustration, maybe as a coping mechanism and as a message to the administration.

A week later I got a call at home from one of the captains.

"Jeff, have you seen today's *Herald*? Be in the deputy chief's office after roll call."

Pete and I were both there. It wasn't too bad; I think the deputy chief saw the humor but missed the message. We wanted to deal with crime, not homeowners trying to save their landscaping.

***

On one of my days off, Pete was working zone three, my regular zone, and he was dispatched to reports of loud music coming from an apartment.

Any disturbance call required two officers to respond, a primary and a backup. More often than not, the primary would cancel the backup on such a routine, nonviolent call, but on this call, either Pete did not cancel his backup or the backup officer went anyway.

When Pete knocked on the door, a bullet crashed through the cheap wooden door and hit him in the back of the head.

The backup officer said Pete was standing off to one side, just as we were trained. An officer never stands directly in front of a door or window. But the man inside was also off to one side, sitting on his sofa. The knock made him angry, and he shot blindly at the door. Pete went down, and the other officer pulled him away from the front door and called for rescue and additional officers.

My friends on the scene said Pete was fighting fire-rescue as they tried to stabilize him, clawing at hands he could not see.

I went to see him one night in the ICU at Jackson Memorial. I was in uniform, which is like a free pass sometimes, and I walked right in.

Pete was in a special bed, a coma bed, the nurse called it. It oscillated to keep blood clots from forming; it was weird and also painful watching it moving him around. Pete's head and face were so swollen he was unrecognizable. I talked to him for a few minutes, and I prayed. I knew if something like that happened to me, I would want a quick and painless death.

Pete lingered in a coma for a week and mercifully died on November 19, 1992.

I wish I had been working that night. Maybe I could have helped him somehow or maybe I would have gotten the call and stood just a little different or maybe I would have died. So many "maybes." It's called survivor's guilt, and we all get it.

There was another immense funeral for Pete at a different church, the same honor guard, the same politicians, the media, etc. It was all beautiful—but Pete was gone.

He was only 34.

The shooter was convicted of second-degree murder and sentenced to twenty-five years in prison.

Those were the two most significant deaths for me: Emilio and Pete, close friends killed in the line of duty, but there would be more deaths and more funerals to come.

CHAPTER 25

TRAFFIC CRASHES

"Don't follow too close and always wear your seat belts," I tell my kids, and they roll their eyes at me. I tell them this because I've seen things they haven't, things I don't want to tell them yet.

I handled more traffic crashes than I could ever count, sometimes two or three per shift. Most traffic fatalities are very similar and easy to forget. Two cars collide and someone dies, usually of blunt force trauma. During my career, I probably saw several hundred traffic fatalities. It sounds like a lot, and it is, but even ten per year would be 240 deaths, and I'm sure it was a lot more. Fortunately, a traffic homicide investigator handled most of the fatalities, but I was the officer who got there first—when everything was still fresh and the blood was still flowing, when some of them were still alive and screaming, but died soon after.

Today, if I were in a wreck and dying, it would give me comfort in those last few minutes of life if an officer told me he was going to take care of me, that I was going to be okay. I wouldn't blame him for being wrong.

The wrecks I've written about so far were early in my career, and for that reason they were memorable. The later ones require something odd to trigger a memory, something gut-wrenching like the one titled New Year's Eve. But I have so many I think anyone trying to read them all would lose interest and eventually skip to another page so I'll keep the list short.

Shards of Glass

One sunny afternoon, a young couple rear-ended a car stopped at a red light. The car behind the couple rear-ended their car. Pretty routine in Hialeah but this one was a little different.

I walked up to the mangled car in the middle and found the passenger, a young woman maybe eighteen years old, unconscious in her seat. Her head was leaning to the left and her right eye was facing me. Her face was covered in blood, and amid all this blood, a couple dozen tiny shards of mirrored glass were stuck into her eye and cheekbone, like a pin cushion.

The passenger door's mirror was shattered and covered in blood. On the floorboard, scattered around her feet, were her lipstick and makeup.

She had been leaning out of her window, using the side mirror to put on her makeup. The impact slammed her face into the mirror, and like a cookie cutter, it cut a perfect oval around her eye.

The driver, her boyfriend, had somehow been flung into the backseat. He was also unconscious; I heard later he had died, but the woman lived.

It was an older car, a late seventies Mustang. There were no airbags to save them and neither of them were wearing seat belts.

***

These two victims are the reasons I tell my kids to drive safely and to use their seat belts, and they give me the look—parents know the look I'm talking about.

In my twisted mind, even to this day I can imagine my son or my daughter with those mirrored shards of glass sticking in their eyes.

I still remind them that I love them and to be careful.

I can live with the look.

Seat Belts

I'd been involved in plenty of car chases, and they really weren't like the ones on TV. They are less dramatic, less choreographed, and more chaotic. Amazingly, I never wrecked a car despite sliding around on the vinyl bench seat. Anything on the seat usually ended up on the floorboard, sometimes even the radio, then the officer was totally screwed. Without a seat belt, all I had to hold me in place was the steering wheel.

Speaking of seat belts, Susan, who still wouldn't go out with me at the time, caught me sitting in my patrol car, not wearing a seat belt.

"Why aren't you wearing your seat belt?"

"I hate them," I said sheepishly.

Seat belts were notorious for catching on badges and pens and ripping them off our shirts. I truly hated them, but then and there I promised to wear my seat belt, hoping someday Susan would be impressed. Less than an hour later I was involved a long, high-speed chase that led me all through Miami-Dade County.

An armed robbery was reported at one of the stores in Westland Mall, and one of my zone partners saw a car matching the description of the subject's car and tried to stop it. A chase ensued and I knew it was going to go right past me.

I checked my seat belt and pushed my briefcase and a plastic milk crate I used to store blank reports onto the passenger side floorboards to keep them from sliding around.

With the seat belt on, I felt secure—and ready.

It was a long chase along crowded streets that ended twenty miles later when the driver lost control. He crashed into a building by a Royal Castle.

My brakes were beginning to overheat, a common problem in car chases, and I ended up crushing some of the restaurant's landscaping as I tried to stop.

For those who know the area, the chase started in the parking lot of the mall, which is in the far west end of Hialeah, and it ended at NW 27th Avenue and 79th Street. It was the longest chase I had ever been on; amazingly, no one was injured, and the driver was arrested.

Later that night I saw Susan and she asked about the chase.

"It was exciting!" I told her. "And the seat belt made me feel safer."

"I better never catch you not wearing it!"

***

I lost plenty of pens and had my badge ripped off my shirt a few times by that seat belt, but I never drove without it again.

Seat Belts, Again

I was driving down a quiet residential street at about 4 a.m. A pick-up truck was in front of me, two blocks away. I saw the truck, but I was focused more on the houses around me. I was more interested in crime than traffic.

In front of me I saw a flash of headlights, then a shower of sparks followed by a cloud of dust and smoke as the pick-up truck spun around and overturned. As it spun, the headlights acted like the rotating beacon of a lighthouse, and in their beam, I saw something big fly through the air. I turned on my blue lights and called it in on the radio.

I parked behind the overturned truck and looked inside, but I didn't see the driver. Farther down the road were a crumpled-up car and two people lying motionless in the street.

As I started to run toward them, a man standing in his backyard said, "Officer, I think this man is dead."

Hidden in the dark swale next to the truck was the driver. He was a big man, probably 250 pounds or more, and lying on his back. His chest was oddly flat, and he was definitely not breathing. I checked anyway, but there was no pulse.

As I ran down the street to the other victims, I radioed the dispatcher that I had at least one fatality and maybe more.

The man and woman on the asphalt were unconscious; they were banged up pretty bad, but they lived. Rescue's response was always quick, and sure enough, they arrived and took them to the hospital.

What I saw fly out of the truck was the driver, who was ejected through the passenger window. When the truck overturned, it crushed him. I was amazed at how quickly such a big man had been thrown out of such a small window.

He would be alive today if he had been wearing a seat belt.

The Ninja

For weeks, seemingly every night, officers had tried to stop a speeding motorcyclist racing through the streets of Hialeah. He rode a red Kawasaki Ninja and always wore a red full face helmet.

The biker would flee as soon as an officer tried to stop him, often at speeds over one hundred miles per hour. The chases were quickly abandoned by the officer or canceled by a supervisor as it was just too dangerous. I tried one night with the same results.

It was hard to abandon the chase—it felt like I was letting the guy win some type of sporting event, but in the end, I knew my life, his life, and the lives of everybody around us were at stake.

Late one night we were called to the scene of an accident on Okeechobee Road. Okee is a long stretch of open road with little traffic after midnight. I wasn't dispatched, but when I heard it involved a red motorcycle, I headed toward it. The rider had already been transported by paramedics by the time I arrived, but the bike was still there.

It was apparent the driver had been speeding, lost control, and hit a utility pole. The bike was a crumpled mess spread over several hundred feet, and it was hard to tell what type of bike it was, but enough of the red plastic parts were there to know it was a red Ninja. Near a big pool of blood, I found a red, full face helmet.

The rider died before reaching the hospital. We don't know if it was the same Ninja, but there were no more nightly chases.

Tractor Trailer vs Man

It was early in the evening but still daylight when I was dispatched to a hit-and-run accident involving a pedestrian and a tractor trailer.

When I arrived, there was no sign of an accident.

A witness described seeing a male pedestrian standing on the corner trying to cross the street. As the tractor trailer made a right turn, it hit the victim, who was then trapped between two of the truck's rear wheels.

The witness said the man was revolving around and around as the truck dragged the man down the street for several blocks and eventually out of his sight.

He pointed to the section of the street where it started—some blood, flesh, and bits of clothing marked the point of impact; the trail of gore continued for a hundred yards then diminished until it was untraceable.

An accident investigator arrived and we shut down several blocks. As the sun set, crime scene technicians lit up the street with their big, portable lights to search for more evidence. We never found the truck or the remains of the pedestrian.

As gruesome as it sounds, there wasn't much to see. It was knowing what happened to the man and knowing some trucker knew what he had done and fled anyway that frustrated me for months. I kept waiting to hear that somehow the truck driver was found but he never was.

The Flashing Light

One night I was transporting a drunken prisoner to city hall for processing. Clear Plexiglas separated me from the back seat so I could see him; he was a happy drunk sitting quietly, looking out the window. It was near the end of my shift, about one in the morning. I didn't want to be late and go into overtime—supervisors didn't like signing overtime cards.

I was driving on one of the main arteries in the city, and at that time of night, many of the traffic signals switched to flashing lights: yellow for the primary street and red for the secondary. In Hialeah, and most of the country, flashing red means stop. In some countries, it must mean something else because as I approached a flashing yellow light, another car was approaching the flashing red, and it was clear the driver wasn't stopping or even slowing.

It was already too late for me to brake; my prisoner saw it, too. He was screaming like he was on fire, and I couldn't blame him. His hands were cuffed behind his back, and his face was about two feet from the Plexiglas. When I hit the brakes at 45 miles per hour, it sent his face into the divider, then I broadsided the other car.

There was no airbag in my vehicle; it was a 1985 Dodge Diplomat. Only my seat belt (thank you, Susan) probably kept me alive. I was knocked out or just stunned for a minute and when I came to, I was confronted by screaming from the prisoner in the back seat, loud noises from the destroyed engine, steam and smoke through the vents, and a man banging on my window.

As I tried to figure out what the hell had just happened, I ignored the man. When I realized I had just had a pretty bad wreck, I grabbed the microphone off the dashboard to raise dispatch with my unit number, but no one answered. I was confused. I couldn't understand why no one was answering me, and I thought maybe the radio was damaged, too.

I needed to get out of the smoking car. The engine and fan were making lots of noises, so I turned off the engine, but the prisoner was still screaming.

Then I looked again through my driver's window at the man still standing there, holding his left arm.

"Are you okay, officer?"

Hell no! I thought.

The man's forearm was fractured and bent at an odd angle, but he was still trying to help me out of my car with his good arm. My doorframe was crushed, and it took both of us to open it.

It had been probably a minute or two at most since the impact, and I was starting to think coherently again. I checked the prisoner. His nose was broken, and one eye was swollen shut but nothing serious. I pulled him from the back seat and sat him on the sidewalk.

I heard sirens coming from every direction. *Are they coming for me? Did they hear me on the radio after all?* What a glorious sound those sirens made. I was soon surrounded by my fellow officers.

Fire-rescue took the other driver to the hospital, a midnight shift officer took my prisoner to Ward D (the prison section of Jackson Memorial Hospital), and someone else brought me back to the station. I was sore as hell the next several days from the seat belt but otherwise okay.

***

Later they told me our dispatcher heard someone screaming 3-17, serious accident, on the records frequency, a separate channel, and it took them a minute to get to the records console. I had been running a records check a few minutes earlier and had never switched back to the main channel. The dispatcher had recognized my voice, knew where I was headed, and sent everyone looking for me.

The men and women in communications are often overlooked when it comes to law enforcement. Living with Susan, I know the stresses and complexity of their job, and I can never say enough about them. They save more people with their competence than they will ever know.

I do slow down a little more now when I approach a flashing yellow light.

Superman and the Train

I was on my way to court in downtown Miami, and the afternoon rush hour had already begun. Right on schedule, at the worst possible time, a long, slow-moving train cut our city in half. Traffic came to a complete stop in all six lanes of Lejeune Road. Then the train came to a complete stop, and I knew I was going to be late for court.

After twenty minutes, the train began to creep along and finally the red caboose rolled across the street, and the automatic arms rose. I was about twenty cars back in the southbound lanes, which still weren't moving, so I had a bird's-eye view of what was about to happen. The first northbound vehicle I saw was a motorcycle, and the rider was accelerating hard right at me—he was hauling ass. What he didn't see was the big Ford LTD coming across Lejeune Road from a side street.

I watched helplessly as the motorcycle hit the car's rear quarter panel so hard it spun the heavy car in a 360-degree circle.

The motorcyclist was airborne now, flying without the bike like Superman, and he was still coming right at me. He hit the ground and tumbled a few times and came to a stop next to my driver's door.

I jumped out and called for fire-rescue. The kid was moaning, and I saw lots of road rash on his arms, then I saw his left hand. His entire hand had separated from his wrist, and his forearm bones were about even with the center of his palm. There was no blood, and his skin was red and swollen but unbroken. I couldn't imagine an injury like that was possible.

The kid kept asking about his bike, and I told him, "Don't worry about the bike; it's fine—just don't look at your hand." But of course he did, then the screaming started.

It took fire-rescue a while this time, a result of the train traffic, but they eventually came and took him away.

I had to wait for another officer to arrive and write the report, and I was late for court.

Train #2

It was four in the morning, and I was working a double shift. A traffic accident involving a tractor trailer and a train was dispatched on Okeechobee Road and 21st Street. In Hialeah, Okeechobee Road is part of US 27, the main trucking route through Dade County.

The streets were quiet. There was no traffic, and I couldn't help but wonder how a tractor trailer truck could collide with a train so early in the morning.

The eerie yellow glow of sodium vapor streetlights lit up the accident scene where another officer had already arrived. I stepped out of my car into a river of diesel fuel flowing away from the wreck. It stank, but there was nowhere else to park the car, and I was worried about the other officer. I kept walking and hoped there wouldn't be a fire.

The scene was a mess. The tractor trailer had hit the slow or stopped train so hard it knocked several loaded train cars off the tracks. The truck's cab was crushed; the sheet metal intrusion must have been eight feet or more. The first officer told me there were two dead men inside the cab. I didn't look in. I didn't feel like seeing what I knew was in there.

The railroad warning crossbars had disintegrated in the collision. Bits and pieces were embedded in the truck's grille and the side of a train car, indicating they were down and working at the time of the crash.

The investigator thought the truck driver had probably fallen asleep and hit the train at full speed. The truck's passenger was in the sleeper section of the cab. Both men died instantly.

Train #3

In the middle of the night, a drunken man who came from a nearby bar needed to sleep. The area around him was overgrown with weeds and full of trash, so he found the cleanest place to lie down— between the steel rails of a train track near Hialeah Park. The vibrating tracks of an approaching train must have woken him, and he lifted his head just in time for the train to hit him in the face.

The conductor had seen the man in the engine's light but was unable to stop. Although the train was moving slowly as it approached the rail yard a mile away, it still took several hundred yards to come to a complete stop. The conductor radioed his headquarters, and they called us.

The train's crew and a few of us searched the tracks. It took us awhile to find the man, but we eventually did. Incredibly, he was still between the rails, his face was bleeding profusely, and his nose was ripped free, hanging from a piece of skin still attached to his forehead.

We thought he was dead at first. But he was actually asleep, and he was mad as hell when we woke him up.

Although his wounds were gruesome, they were superficial, and he lived.

Train #4

I worked the scene of another wreck involving a train and a pickup truck one afternoon. Fortunately, I was spared the visual nightmare as I only had to reroute traffic for a few hours while the accident investigator and CSX railroad employees worked the actual crash.

I could see the truck from my intersection but never got close to it. I knew the driver had been decapitated, and his head was in the bed of the truck. I was spared that sight, but knowing it had happened and hearing about it afterward has stuck with me all these years.

I spoke to the accident investigator just the other day about this wreck. We were having lunch after attending a friend's funeral. As he described the scene, I noticed him look away and his demeanor changed. I knew he was reliving that day, the way I relive mine.

***

Today and most every day, I drive over a train track to get to town. All too often, crossing those tracks or the smell of diesel fuel triggers this memory. This scene, or one of the other three train wrecks I've written about, pops up and plays like a thirty-second commercial each time as I relive them.

Spectators vs Responders

We never know when something big is going to happen, and sometimes it happens right in front of us. When something does happen, we have a decision to make, one we have to live with forever. Do we watch or do we help?

I was in morning rush hour traffic on West 84th Street. About a hundred yards ahead of me was a sudden burst of smoke and dust, followed by the red flashes of brake lights. I put my blue lights on, drove off the road and onto the swale to see what had happened.

Just ahead was an intersection with a small side street. In the middle of the intersection, against the concrete curb, a motorcycle was on its side; the driver, motionless, was next to it.

I ran over to him, and a woman joined me. As I got down on my knees, I saw the man was unconscious. His eyes were wide-open, staring vacantly into the sky; he was jerking, and gasping for air. A closer look revealed the bike's handlebar had perforated his helmet and was deep inside his skull.

The motorcycle's engine was still running and gas was dripping from the tank. I worried it would catch fire with the victim pinned to it. I found the key and turned it off. Pulling the handlebar out of his brain was out of the question—it wouldn't help him and even the thought of it made me queasy.

The woman next to me said, "I'm a nurse at Palmetto Hospital, is there anything I can help you with?"

"I don't think it will make a difference but try and hold his helmet still," I said.

Then, as if things weren't bad enough, I heard someone screaming behind me.

On the other side of the guardrail was the steep bank of the canal that ran parallel with the road. A man was almost hidden in the weeds that choked the bank; his legs and most of his torso were underwater. He was slowly slipping deeper, and he couldn't stop himself because his arms looked broken.

"I have to get that guy out of the water," I told the nurse. "Hold him still, fire-rescue is on the way."

She seemed nervous. I don't know what type of nurse she was, but I don't think she was used to dealing with injuries like this. But she was down on her knees holding this man's helmet while everyone else sat in their cars.

I crawled down the bank, grabbed the collar of the man's

jacket, and dragged him all the way up to level ground. He screamed in pain each time I pulled on him, but I couldn't leave him where he was. When I got him to flatter ground, I noticed one of his legs was broken, too. Fortunately, fire-rescue arrived.

The rescue lieutenant looked at the driver with the handlebar stuck in his brain then looked at me. "This one's a goner," he said.

I noticed the man had stopped convulsing.

The nurse finally let go of his helmet and stood up. She watched the paramedics work on the second man while I started the investigation.

"Thanks for everything," I told her. I called for a traffic homicide officer and two more officers to help me redirect traffic.

Our investigation revealed a car ran the stop sign at the side street, and the bike broadsided it. The driver of the car fled the scene. Fortunately, another motorist witnessed the accident, followed the car, and eventually forced it off the road several miles away.

The dead motorcylist and his passenger were two young men on their way to work.

I never saw the driver of the car that fled; I wished I could have described the man's injuries to him, face-to-face.

***

This occurred during morning rush hour traffic on a busy street, yet not one person got out of their car to help me, except the nurse. I cannot understand it! How can anyone sitting in their car watch this happen and not want to try and help?

This was the late 90s when most cell phones didn't have cameras. Today, I believe most of those drivers would have been standing outside their cars trying to get the best view and recording the man's death, hoping their video would be on the news or go viral on YouTube. It happens on TV every day, and it makes me sick.

It seems it takes a different kind of person to get involved these days, to get their hands dirty, like nurses and doctors and first responders do.

Traffic Enforcement

Many people think of a police officer as that cop on the side of the road who's running radar, trying to write a ticket, and spoil their trip to grandma's house. Can't they find something better to do? Go fight real crime, officer!

I don't think I ever enjoyed writing traffic tickets; it wasn't something I ever looked forward to when I went to work each day. Writing a ticket was a pain in the ass, to be honest; however, it's probably easier now thanks to computers. True, there were times when it was gratifying, when I hoped maybe the ticket would someday save a life, but it was never fun.

The officer who's pointing the radar gun at traffic on the highway is the same officer who has to clean up the mess, the blood, and the death caused by speeding drivers every day. Those speed limit signs aren't meant to make the trip to the store any slower—they're meant to increase the likelihood of surviving a wreck, which will inevitably happen one day.

When I tell some of my new friends I was tough on drunk drivers, I get "the look." The blinking of the eyes, the moment they were about to say something but changed their mind. Cops know the look I'm talking about.

I received an award one year from MADD, Mothers Against

Drunk Drivers. DUI arrests aren't fun; they were an even bigger pain in the ass with all the paperwork and procedures I had to follow, and I was lucky if the drunk didn't puke in the back seat of my patrol car.

I've been hit and injured twice by drunk drivers, and I will never forget some of the horrific traffic fatalities I saw.

Let's talk about New Year's Eve.

CHAPTER 26

NEW YEAR'S EVE

This story begins with the death of one person, and ends in the death of three people several years later.

In South Florida, and maybe in other parts of the country, people celebrate the New Year by shooting their firearms at midnight. Most of the community is outraged by the amount of lead flying through the air during those first thirty minutes of the year, but it still happens every year.

Sometime in the mid-80s, a young mother and her family were at the dining table celebrating New Year's Eve when a bullet crashed through the window and struck her in the head, killing her instantly. This was the third or fourth consecutive New Year's Eve fatality caused by stray gunfire in South Florida.

This tragic and sensational death played out in the media for several days. I didn't see or hear details about the crime scene, but in my mind I pictured a young mother, face down in her dinner plate, surrounded by her horrified children.

That night, like the New Year's Eve before, I had taken cover with most of the night shift in an underground parking lot. Once the shooting died down, we began responding to the reports of damaged vehicles, bullets landing inside people's homes, and so forth. It was a well-founded fear to be out patrolling during those first thirty minutes of the New Year. And should an officer actually catch someone firing a gun in celebration and make an arrest, it was a simple misdemeanor usually thrown out by the state's attorney. At worst, the offender would pay a fine, there would be no criminal record, and they would get their gun back. But the officer was criticized, by supervisors and fellow officers, for wasting valuable time.

Regardless, I came to a decision after that young mother was killed—the next New Year's Eve, I would hunt and arrest as many of those shooters as I could. The next year I made the first arrest.

The man was alone in the swale of his front yard and never saw me walk up. It was probably a stupid move on my part, walking up to an armed man who was doing what so many others were doing, but I wasn't thinking that way. I wore a bulletproof vest, I had a shiny badge and a .45 in my hand; I felt invulnerable.

After the arrest, I transported the man to jail, which took about two hours. So for those two hours, my zone partners worked without me.

The next year I arrested another man, but instead of transporting him, I confiscated his gun and had him sign the arrest form with a PTA or "promise to appear" in court. I arrested another man a few minutes later.

I did the same the following year. My naïve intent was to get the word out that there was a price to pay for stupidity and endangering others.

The next summer I was promoted to sergeant and spent two years in communications before getting back to patrol. Back on the road, the very next New Year's Eve started just like the rest of them, a lot of gunfire and very few fireworks.

Sure enough, I heard someone firing in an alleyway nearby. I parked the car and walked down the dark alley, which lit up with the flashes of gunfire. I crept up on the man and confronted him. Then things went bad.

The man ran back inside his open gate, and I tackled him in his backyard in front of his family and about twenty party guests. I called for backup, as these drunken partygoers were angry. After all, I was arresting their host, and they felt he wasn't hurting anyone.

I got him handcuffed and led him right through his own living room and out the front door of his house as other officers arrived to help. Those officers had probably been taking shelter in the underground parking lot and didn't seem real happy to see me. Because I was a sergeant, they knew one of them was probably going to have to transport my prisoner to jail.

As I started the paperwork, the alert tone sounded on the radio. It was a 3-17, a traffic accident with serious injuries, and it was in my zone.

I sent my backup officers to the accident and pulled the man out of the car, told him I was giving him a break, and he wouldn't be going to jail this night. I had him sign the promise to appear, and he apologized profusely.

Before I could get back into my car, the first responding officers were arriving at the accident, and I knew it was a bad one from the sound of their voices on the radio.

Within a few minutes, I was on the scene at the intersection of East 10th Avenue and 49th Street. A small car was fully engulfed in flames, and a van with massive front end damage was behind it. The smell of burning human flesh was overpowering. The fire was so intense even the asphalt street was on fire.

An officer described one of the victim's screams, and I watched his face crumple with grief. The small car was occupied by a young couple who had stopped at a red light. The van, full of drunks celebrating the New Year, was speeding downhill on an overpass and rear-ended the car. The drunks were uninjured.

A passerby said he tried to get the couple out of the car, but it was so damaged and on fire he couldn't get their seat belts off. He said the woman was unconscious and her hair was already on fire. The man was alert but unable to get out—he was the one screaming.

A fire engine arrived in minutes and put the fire out. Once it had cooled, I looked in at the bodies, and it was difficult to tell which one was the male and which one was the female. Their clothes and hair had burned away; their skin was charred black. Most of the flesh on their faces and hands had burned away, leaving just the gruesome skulls and skeletal finger bones.

It was the underwire from a bra on one body that told me which one was the woman. I can see them still—side by side.

I heard the following day the woman was pregnant. I can imagine their joy learning they were going to be parents, just a young couple out celebrating a new year, a new life.

It is this picture I see when I remember this call, and I remember it every New Year's Eve.

The other driver was charged with three counts of vehicular manslaughter. He was found guilty and sent to prison.

***

I never arrested another person for celebrating with gunfire. It was a useless, wasted effort, and I realized it would never make a difference anyway. Every New Year's Eve since, I pay a small price for my naïveté—I think about this crash, and I wonder if those officers coming to assist me with my arrest could have saved these victims instead.

CHAPTER 27

SUICIDES

"A single death is a tragedy, a million deaths is a statistic."

– Joseph Stalin

As a patrol officer and as a detective, I've seen and investigated many suicides. They are far more common than most people are aware, and the methods are usually split between using a gun, hanging, and overdosing on drugs. Sometimes the victim will leave a note and the investigation is short, just long enough to be sure there is no chance of foul play.

The medical examiner has the final say on the cause of death, and some cases will remain unclassified forever. For example, the death of a drug user who overdosed could have been accidental, a suicide, or even a homicide. Sometimes the cause of death may take weeks or months to determine as the medical examiner waits for drug screening results or the final report from an investigator. I'm sure those are frustrating times for the deceased's family members.

A Simple Hanging

Unlike the hanging on Halloween years ago, this hanging was

pretty nondescriptive. I found a man hanging in his own closet. It was a simple closet with a bifold door and a clothes rod. Using his belt as a slipknot around his neck, he let his knees bend, slowly cutting off the flow of blood until he passed out. Then gravity took over, and he probably died a painless death. I say painless because this is not the strangling type of death from hanging oneself from a tree. That is a different death entirely—the victim remains conscious and fights to breathe.

I can't tell you how old he was, middle-aged probably. It's an image that just won't focus in my mind, like seeing something in my peripheral vision. I can't recall what he was wearing either, and I never thought about it, ever—until recently.

The reality was, once the detective arrived, I wrote a simple report detailing what I did and what I saw. This report was generic, as the detective took care of all the minute, emotional details.

A call like this took about forty-five minutes, start to finish. I would go back into service and more than likely be dispatched to something else equally forgettable. The entire shift would often be spent going from call to call, leaving little time to think about how these calls affected me, or might affect me in the future.

Someone recently suggested I needed to add more emotions to stories like this, and I can understand how that may seem. Here I am, talking about a dead man hanging in his closet, and all I can write is a single paragraph.

After I posted this story on Facebook, my friend and former coworker, Edward L. Beyer Jr, responded with this:

Jeff, we could never survive these calls if we didn't detach ourselves of the reality of what we see. At least you found them quick, and not days later. As Rawcliffe once remarked, "The memories get locked away, and it's better to not let them out." But of course, over the years they seem to find their way out on their own and manifest [in]our psyche in different ways.

Ed hit the nail on the head. Before I retired I had most of these memories locked away. I seldom found myself sitting on the couch thinking of any of these victims or stewing in some type of depression. That stewing in depression started years later, maybe because the numbness, the exposure from the constant horrors and stresses, had worn off and now I was reliving these moments without the shield of detachment.

Traditional Hanging

On another call, an elderly man suffering from poor health hung himself in his backyard. He tied a rope around an old dead tree and put his head through a noose and stepped off a small stool.

He was about a foot off the ground, and his neck stretched grotesquely from his own body weight. He was probably conscious for a minute and struggled with the rope as he died.

This man lived alone, and a neighbor saw the body and called it in. I never saw or spoke to any family, and today this scene has little effect on me. I see the backyard, the old dead tree, the rope, the man's stretched-out neck, but not much else.

A typical report would be something like this:

> *I arrived at the dispatched location and found the victim hanging from a tree by a rope. The victim was deceased, and I notified the detective bureau. Detective John Doe responded. NOI. (No other information.)*

The detective's report would have been much more descriptive; he would have interviewed family members and neighbors. He would have requested the crime scene unit and a medical examiner, and eventually, they would have determined the cause of death.

This detective would also remember if the dead man's loved ones cried as he delivered the death notification. He would learn all there was to know about the man's misery and despair, and what drove him to kill himself.

I remember this call, but I don't dream about the victim.

Another coworker involved in this suicide case also responded to my Facebook post and his comment proved one of my earlier points—as mundane and routine as this hanging was to me at the time, it was tragic for someone else.

Jeff, that was across the street from my old house, which my ex-wife and son still live in. The man was the father of my son's best friend. I arrived sometime after he was found and transported. By the way, his sons…cut that tree down later that night.

In my story about the hanging on Halloween night, I injected a little humor and a little irony into a horrible event. Humor was often our only coping mechanism. We had to find a way to deflect the rawness. It was death—it was suicide—up close and personal. We had to touch it every day and go home each night and pretend it never happened.

***

In this next case, I think about these two officers, my friends and coworkers, who dealt with the same man two weeks apart, and I try to imagine what they cannot forget. These are their comments to one of my Facebook posts.

George F.: *Jeff, the one I relive STILL is the man I saved in 1983 or 1984 with John A., and Sgt. Johnny W. in an upstairs apartment in SE Hialeah. The wife and 3 Pampers-ridden little kids were in the home.*

Bedsheets were wrapped around the man's neck [and he was hanging] in his closet. I cut him down, Johnny did mouth to mouth, I pumped his chest until rescue arrived. Yep, WE SAVED HIM, although the sheet DID NOT snap his neck, it did suffocate him. Asshole came back 2 weeks later, killed everyone, himself included.

I edited his comment a bit, and I can feel his frustration as he typed. He saved this man's life one night, had him Baker Acted for a psychological evaluation, and some doctor must have thought he was okay and sent him home.

Here's the other officer's comment—he was called to the same apartment two weeks later:

Jeff, funny (not in a humorous manner) how I remember details much like U do. I rarely dream about them, but certain stimuli spark the memory strong and hard while others, just as horrid, are blacked out of my memory banks. I know I was there; I know I did or saw certain things but have no real memory of the details. They are completely blacked out, like the man whose wife was leaving him so he killed all their children in their home then committed suicide.

We were having a SWAT Training Day; we arrived very quickly and made an entry in short order. As SWAT Commander I was the last one through the door. I know I looked at all the bodies, noticed all the blood trails through the house where he chased down his 3- and 4-year-old kids and gunned them down before turning the gun on himself. I can't remember who the sergeant leading the team was, the number of children or sexes, or any graphic details.

So the first officer went home one night feeling the euphoria of saving a man's life. What a high that must have been! Then two weeks later the same man came back and killed his wife and children and committed suicide.

I talked to George today and asked him how it felt when he heard about all the deaths. "Jeff, just one word—betrayed."

I'm not sure if he was referring to God or to life in general, but he said what we all say when someone asks us how we're doing. *"I'm okay."*

Until I began dating Susan, I lived alone and there was never anyone at home to talk to. Not that I ever felt I needed to *talk* about any of the calls. More often than not I was exhausted and was asleep a few minutes after getting home.

But there were calls I *thought* about all the time; I would fall asleep thinking about them and wake up thinking about them. They are my photographic memories, the ones I still dream about.

My Last Hanging

This last hanging was different. A maintenance man servicing the street lamps on one of our highways found a man hanging and called the police.

This street lamp is a common type along major highways. It's tall, fifty or sixty feet tall, and to change the bulbs, a worker lowers the fixture with a pulley system and swaps the bulbs out at ground level. The base of this particular tower was in a heavily wooded area not visible from the street. It's like the Amazon jungle with all the bugs and heat and humidity.

John, one of my senior detectives, and I made our way to the scene and found the victim completely skeletonized.

He wasn't hanging; he was almost sitting, leaning against the tree with a rope around his neck. Like the suicide victim in the closet, he had let his own weight and the noose cut off the blood and oxygen to his brain until he passed out and gravity did the rest. The passage of time had stretched him out enough to put him in this sitting position.

He was wearing a suit, or maybe it was just a jacket and dress pants. His bleached, skeletal arm bones stuck out from the sleeves of his dark jacket, and there was a watch on his wrist. Like his wrists, the white leg bones showed at the cuffs of his pants and disappeared into his socks and shoes.

His wallet was either in his lap or nearby, and we found a Florida ID card with his name. He lived down the street and had been reported missing for three or four months.

To step back and remove all emotion, this would look like a set in a horror movie—but it was the end of a man suffering from family stresses, a human being who had given up on life.

This hanging was near the end of my career, and I can't even guess how many suicides I had dealt with already, but that last sentence shows me I hadn't completely lost my empathy for a victim.

The Right Place #1

Sometimes I was in the right place, but I wished I wasn't. There is a Right Place #2, but it's not about death. It's about life.

One evening I was parked in the grassy swale of an elementary school catching up on paperwork when the alert tone sounded—the sound I both dreaded and loved. Something important was coming, and I could feel the beginnings of an adrenaline rush. The call was a 3-30, a shooting. The "3" means it's in progress, or there's a victim down. This shooting was in my zone, but they sent two of my zone partners. Then the dispatcher said the address—the house was right down the street. I could see it from where I was parked. I hit the gas and was in the driveway within seconds, but as I arrived, the dispatcher changed the call to a possible suicide.

The neighborhood was made up of new townhomes that all looked alike. Each had a small front yard with just enough room to park a single car. An older man was in one of the yards, waving his arms at me. He ran inside the townhome, and I ran in behind him.

It was a small, modest room that was both the kitchen and living area. An older woman was standing alone in the kitchen. I ignored her and turned my attention to a small, thin girl with light brown skin and straight, shoulder-length, dark brown hair who sat on the sofa, motionless. She was wearing jeans and a white shirt, her head was tilted back, and her eyes were open as if she were staring at the ceiling. Tiny beads of perspiration dotted her forehead. A small revolver was on the cushion, next to her hand, and there was a distinct smell of gun smoke.

I was looking for a head wound and didn't see the hole in her chest at first—but there it was—a small black .38-caliber hole in her white shirt, a single drop of blood next to it. I placed my fingers on her neck, hoping for a pulse, but there was none. She was still warm though, and I thought, it was such a small hole and with so little blood lost, maybe she would live.

I lifted her shirt to see the wound. It was a contact wound, which means the barrel was pressed against her skin. The bullet went through part of her bra and was just to the left of the center in her sternum. Like the hole in her blouse, the hole in her sternum was also black, seared by the heat or the soot, but it revealed the cream-colored bone along the edges. And as if that image wasn't bad enough, the bullet broke through the underwire in her bra and forced one end of it into the hole as well. The metal was a dull grey but had a shiny scratch from the bullet. The end of the wire was jagged; I knew a piece of it had been ripped off and was inside her.

All of this took about fifteen seconds, then I sat next to her, knowing she was dead and nothing I could do would save her.

I radioed the dispatcher and said the girl was dead, and I would need a detective to respond. I sat in the kitchen with the woman I thought was her mother, who showed me a handwritten note and told me the story.

She didn't speak fluent English, but she was able to tell me that in the last day or so, she learned the girl had been dating someone she disapproved of and prohibited her from seeing the boy again.

The woman and her husband, who I learned later were her aunt and uncle, had gone out for a few minutes, and as they arrived home, they heard the gunshot. They ran inside and found the girl on the couch and the note on the table.

They were, of course, devastated. Some people scream and convulse in their grief, but these two were the other kind, numb and in shock, like they had died as well.

I can't recall everything in that note, but it started with *I accepted you both as my mother and father...*

This suicide happened just days after Susan and I got the first picture of our soon-to-be daughter, Sarah. She was two years old, a cute little Colombian girl with light brown skin and dark brown hair. The coincidence was not lost on me—this young girl had chosen to end her life as Sarah was about to come into mine.

Christmas Eve

> *Suicides spike between Thanksgiving and New Year's Day. The experts say the victims see everyone around them happy; after all, it's the holidays—and their depression intensifies.*

It was Christmas Eve, and I was dispatched to a 44, a suicide.

I arrived and found a sixteen-year-old girl lying in her bed with a gunshot wound to her right temple. A black .38-caliber revolver was on the pink and white flowered sheets, a few inches away from her right hand. I couldn't help but notice the stark, disturbing contrast between the black gun and the flowers on the sheets.

I moved the gun away from her hand, and also away from her mother, who was standing behind me. The last thing I needed was a clearly distraught mother picking it up and killing herself, too.

Although the girl was half-covered by the floral sheet, she was fully clothed, and her long, dark brown hair covered most of her face. She was still very much alive, but not in a good way.

The young girl was convulsing and gagging as her brain forced her lungs to breathe. It's hard to describe what that sounds like—a deep wet noise similar to vomiting or the gasping for breath when someone's been underwater too long and breaks to the surface.

Her hands and fingers were curled inward, and her feet extended outward, like her muscles were cramping, all signs of a severe brain injury. Most people have seen the hands and feet of someone with cerebral palsy: it looks the same.

It took a while for rescue to arrive, and there was little I could do while I waited. She vomited again, and I grabbed her arm and leg and pulled her toward me and onto her side so she didn't choke on her own puke. She was unresponsive, her brown eyes unfocused, and there was no recognition in them, no tears, no emotions, no sign at all that she was aware of what was happening to her.

Now that she was on her side, the entry wound was visible; a dark hole in her thick, dark brown hair, matted with red blood, and surprisingly, there was no exit wound.

The girl's mother was still standing behind me. She never spoke to me, she just kept repeating, *"Dios mio, Dios mio."* My God, my God.

Her eyes were red, and I could tell she had been crying, but there were no tears, just her red, watery eyes glancing back and forth between her daughter and me, constantly wringing her hands as if she were washing them under a faucet.

A second daughter was in an adjoining bedroom, crying. The mother began pacing back and forth in the small hallway between the two bedrooms, still looking at her convulsing daughter then at me. I wasn't sure what she was thinking—hoping, maybe—or why I wasn't doing more for her daughter.

Through the window in the girl's room, which overlooked the front yard, neighbors stared in at me.

Rescue finally arrived, and the guys did what they could to stabilize her, then transported her to Jackson Memorial Hospital.

I learned the girl's older sister had discovered she had been having sex and was about to tell their mother. This was a middle-class Hispanic family, and I wondered then if it was a moral stigma or a religious issue, or if there was a dominant father figure she was afraid of.

But how bad could that conversation have been? An argument probably, an awkward week or two around the house, and she would have had her whole life ahead of her—but instead, she shot herself in the head.

Maybe this young girl thought she would leave the ultimate guilt trip on her sister or show her love for whatever boy she had been seeing. But the truth was—she was dead—and she will never know.

I never spoke to the older sister; I never really saw anything more than her feet through the open doorway of her bedroom. Fire-rescue and a detective were in the house, and I wanted to be out of their way.

I sat at the family's kitchen table and started my report. I can't remember a single item in that kitchen, or any other part of the house. The memory begins and ends at the threshold of that bedroom door.

She died twelve hours later.

***

Years later when my daughter was fourteen, she and my son were in a church youth group that met every Wednesday. They had been working on a skit for weeks and were going to perform it for the congregation the following Sunday.

That morning she was excited and nervous, and Susan and I were, too.

The skit was about a troubled girl and her interactions with her friends. I was in the middle of the second row, watching as my daughter—the troubled girl—pulled out a realistic toy pistol and held it to her head.

I was instantly back in that dying girl's bedroom and that girl was my daughter. I was beyond horrified. I felt as if I were paralyzed, which was probably a good thing or I would have jumped up in front of everybody and told them what I thought of their fucking play. Instead, I covered my face and tried not to show how shaken I was.

I never forgave those youth ministers, and although they probably thought their message was a good one, I did not.

In the following weeks, Susan and I noticed our kids were coming home depressed from their Wednesday night meeting.

Their eyes were red and swollen, and it was obvious they had been crying.

"What's happening?" I asked.

At the end of each meeting, the ministers had the kids form a circle and discuss things that had hurt them emotionally: the deaths of loved ones, bullying at school, abusive parents, etc., and each kid felt compelled to share their stories. Again, the ministers might have had good intentions, but I wasn't sending my kids to church to come home crying every night.

Chapter 28

The Staircase Death

A reader once asked me, "How do you prepare yourself as you're responding to a call where someone has died?"

It's a complex and yet a simple answer. I prepared myself for the worst. The worst might be a homicide, and if I was careless, I could be the next victim. I went through a mental checklist—what does the dispatcher know, have I been to this place before, what kind of a neighborhood is it? And I asked myself—are alarm bells going off in my head?

One afternoon I was dispatched to a 45, a dead person.

I arrived to find a neighbor waiting outside for me. The neighbor told me a teenage girl had come home from school, found her front door locked and her father not answering the doorbell. She went to the back of the house and jimmied the locked sliding glass doors and went inside. She found her father dead on the staircase and ran next door to this neighbor's house, who then called the police.

I checked the man for a pulse and found none. His skin was cold, and I knew he had been dead for several hours. There were no apparent signs of foul play, and I called for a detective.

The stairwell was shaped like an L, a ninety degree turn with a small landing in the middle. The victim was upside down on the landing with his back and legs up against the wall and his head and neck bent at an odd angle.

The theory was, he fell and either broke his neck or was knocked out during the fall and was unable to breathe. It's called positional asphyxia, or in plain English, due to his position, he was unable to breathe.

The daughter remained next door while I was there, and I never spoke to her. That was the detective's responsibility. Had I met her, this call would probably have been a depressing one, but it was just another unusual death for me.

Chapter 29

The Diner

A man and his date were seated at a table in a crowded restaurant. As they talked, another diner, a complete stranger who was by himself, got up, plunged his steak knife into the man's back, and walked away.

The victim looked at his date and said, "He stabbed me!" then collapsed and died at the table.

Horrified diners watched the suspect, a man in his mid-twenties, walk calmly through the restaurant, out into the parking lot, and sit on a bus bench. We responded to the call and found the man still sitting on the bench. He was an average-looking guy, a man who wouldn't attract a second look if he were seated at the next table. He was arrested and charged with homicide.

The man suffered from a mental disorder, schizophrenia, and this case never went to trial.

This death happened in real life—not on *CSI: Miami* or *Law and Order* but in an average restaurant. Someone can be sitting in a restaurant enjoying the company of a date one minute—and dead the next. Like a light switch—on and off. That's what sticks with me after all these years, how random life and death can be.

When people with no experience in law enforcement watch a horrible news report of an officer killing or tasing a person with mental illness, they wonder why the police officers had to use such deadly force on someone who was simply mentally ill. They see the victim's loved ones crying on the television, *He was just disturbed, he needed help, and they killed him!* and they're sympathetic.

In my experience, there is no man or woman more dangerous than someone who is mentally ill. Police officers can't reason with them, and they can't negotiate with them. Remember this poor victim sitting with his date having a pleasant dinner the next time a news anchor mentions mental illness. Ted Bundy and Jeffrey Dahmer were both mentally ill, and the two of them killed as many as forty-seven innocent victims.

Chapter 30

Random Events

There are no deaths in these events. Some are tragic, some are humorous, but they are all memorable.

The Old Man and the Sea

I received a call about a man on a bicycle threatening people with a knife, and I found him on the corner of Palm Avenue and 13th Street. This area was once a premier location, back in the 1930s and 40s when Hialeah Park was one of the top horse racing tracks in the country. But now, it was a run-down section of town with old wooden apartment buildings and vacant storefronts. The suspect was an older man but younger than I am now, and he was on a small bike, a red Schwinn Stingray, with a basket on the handlebars.

He saw me and took off down a residential street, peddling as fast as he could. I was in my patrol car, so I followed him until he dropped the bike and ran between two houses.

He had a bit of a lead on me, but he was old and tired, and I wasn't, so I was gaining on him. He turned a corner. I turned the same corner, and he was right there waiting for me—with a long knife in his hand, crouched down like he was ready for a fight.

If I had had my gun in my hand—as I should have, I would

have shot him right there, but I didn't, and I knew I was going to collide with him. I didn't have time to think at all, so on the run at full speed, I stuck my boot out and kicked him in the chest. The knife went flying, and the old guy collapsed.

I'm not Chuck Norris, and I have no martial arts training, but I had been training for more than a year for the 100-meter hurdles. My second Police Olympics were coming up, and another officer and I had been training for the pentathlon. Sticking my boot out just happened, like a reflex.

The knife was a long rusty fish filet knife, and the guy looked like Spencer Tracy in the movie *The Old Man and the Sea.* When I examined the knife after the arrest, I knew I had been lucky; this call could have been really bad. I could have, and probably should have, shot the man. But I also could have been cut up or killed wrestling with him.

I had forgotten about this guy until I saw Ernest Hemingway's name, the author who wrote the book the movie was based on while doing some research. Most of the officers I worked with will remember this guy as a regular nuisance on Palm Avenue in the south end of the city.

***

A friend read this story when I posted it on Facebook. He had been on the board that assigned officers their medals and ribbons for heroic deeds and accomplishments, and he wondered why he never saw a commendation for this call.

"Jeff, I never saw that commendation, that would have qualified you for a Combat Cross."

"There was none," I said.

I learned pretty quickly in patrol that each of my supervisors had different personalities and different work ethics. Some of them I'd never see or hear during my entire shift, and when I did, it was usually bad news.

There were two different times I mentioned something to two different sergeants. One said, "If you want a commendation, write it and I'll sign it." I thought that was BS, and I didn't write anything. The second time I was told, "Good job, but that's what you're paid to do."

I never asked again, but after I was promoted to sergeant, I knew what my officers were doing every day, and I wrote plenty of commendations.

Pepper Spray

Zone one in the south end of Hialeah was a hotbed for crime even before the Mariel Boatlift, and still is. One afternoon two of us were dispatched to two men fighting on Palm Avenue, just a block from where I arrested the Spencer Tracy look-alike months before. We arrived and found one of the guys in front of an old apartment building. He was cooperating, and we were running a computer check on him when he took off and ran into the building.

This guy wasn't old like the guy above, and the two of us were struggling to keep up with him. Our work boots were great for ankle and foot protection or an occasional boot to the chest, but they sucked for running.

I was about ten feet behind the guy with the other officer right behind me. A tiny stream of fluid, like silly string, shot over my shoulder and hit the guy in the back of the head. It was a stream of tear gas-pepper spray, which wouldn't have an effect on the guy unless it hit him in the face and got in the mucous membranes of his mouth and eyes.

However, a fine mist surrounds the stream and I was running right through the mist—and I was breathing hard. It was my mucus membranes that got a full dose, and my face was instantly on fire—like molten lead had been poured into my eyes and throat. Somehow, the three of us ended up in a heap at the end of a hallway.

I couldn't see much and I know I was no help getting the guy back to the sidewalk, but somehow we did it. Fire-rescue arrived to treat the guy, who had gotten a good dose of the spray too.

Rescue poured water over my eyes several times, but I'd been gassed so often I knew it was going to take time to wear off. It's amazing how much mucus the human head can hold. My nose ran like a faucet, and my eyes watered and burned for thirty minutes.

As soon as I could see well enough to drive, I went home and threw the uniform in the washer. When I wore that shirt the next week, I could still feel the spray burning my eyes.

I can laugh about it now, but I wasn't laughing then.

The Gunshot Victim

How many non-first responders have ever seen a gunshot wound in person? Trust me, they all look different. Big guns of course make bigger wounds, but a smaller gun fired close to the victim can be deadly, too. Sometimes the wound is a tiny pinprick, with very little blood and no exit wound. Sometimes they are big, gaping holes that leave shredded tissue and pieces of bone protruding from the wound, and the bleeding can be tremendous. This next case was common, a gunshot wound to the abdomen.

I was dispatched to a shooting on Okeechobee Road. This

section of Okee was known for its seedy bars, prostitutes, sex motels, and run-down and abandoned storefronts. This was a Sunday afternoon, and the area was unusually quiet. The bars were closed, the prostitutes were waiting for the sun to go down, and except for a laundromat, the businesses were all closed.

I pulled into an empty parking lot, where a heavy man was dragging himself across the pavement, using just his arms. His shirt was soaked in blood. There was no one around, no sign of a shooter, and no witnesses. I ran over to him, and he ignored me, still pulling himself across the asphalt—his legs dragging uselessly behind him.

I finally got him to stop, and I rolled him onto his back so I could see the wound. Just below his ribcage was a small bullet hole, but there was a lot of blood coming out of it. I didn't hear the sirens of a fire-rescue truck yet, so I pressed my palm over the hole to stop the bleeding.

I made two mistakes. The first one was not running back to the car and getting a latex glove. The second one was underestimating how painful pressing on a bullet wound might be.

The guy began screaming and pushed himself away from me, but immediately, the bleeding slowed to a faint trickle.

As I knelt next to him, I could feel the heat coming from the black asphalt, then he started dragging himself again, this time in a sitting position, using his arms to lift his butt off the ground and inching backward toward the laundromat.

The man had yet to acknowledge I was even there: no eye contact, no words—nothing. He was solely focused on dragging himself to a small strip of shade next to the building.

Once he was in the shade and propped up against the building, he stopped moving. His skin was pasty white, and he stared vacantly across the parking lot. He was in shock now, and

I watched as his already-big belly grew bigger. He was still bleeding, but now it was internal. It took several minutes for fire-rescue to arrive and in just those few minutes I saw his belly bloat several inches.

Once rescue loaded him up, I searched for witnesses. The only business open was the laundromat, and the several women doing their laundry said they hadn't seen or heard anything. I notified detectives, the crime scene technicians, and once everything was under control, I headed to the hospital. The detectives were now in charge of the scene. All I needed was his name for my report, and I hoped the ER staff had it.

I arrived at Palmetto Hospital, one of our three trauma centers, twenty minutes later. The victim was easy to find, as he was the only one screaming. A nurse said the man wouldn't speak to them either, adding he might be paralyzed from the waist down and his condition was critical.

As I watched the trauma team work, one of the nurses held a long tube attached to a canister that looked like a mini-vacuum cleaner. Without administering anesthesia, she stuck the tube into the guy's side and blood immediately flowed into the canister. The sound of the man's screams was now unbearable, and I left the room.

Later, the nurse told me the man was in shock, his blood pressure was dropping, and anesthesia could have killed him. That tube was meant to relieve the pressure off his heart and lungs.

I heard he lived, although paralyzed, but refused to cooperate with the detectives.

Sid

> *The PR-24 looks like a regular nightstick but has a handle. It was made famous by William Shatner on the TV show T. J. Hooker. In the hands of a skilled martial artist, it's probably a formidable weapon, but for the average officer, it was useless and soon every department stopped using them.*

I was transporting a prisoner to the Dade County Jail one night. When transporting prisoners, it was a departmental policy that the officer does not deviate on the way to the jail for any reason, but I was sure there were exceptions, and I was about to make one.

Another officer, Sid, had been dispatched to a domestic violence call. He canceled his backup, which was his first mistake. When he arrived, the domestic was over. One of the parties had left the scene, but Sid decided to run a background check on the man who was still on the scene. Turned out the man had an open bench warrant.

Sid was not a real physical guy, and the man resisted the arrest. Sid pulled out his PR-24, but the man took it from him and threw it aside.

Sid radioed for a backup, and no one responded. My route to the jail was going to take me within a few blocks of this call. I was hoping someone would come on the air and back him up, but no one did. I turned to head toward the call, and as I did the officer yelled, "Shots fired! I shot him in the leg!"

"Shit!" I was really pushing the car hard now; the prisoner was sliding all over the back seat, and I was beginning to worry about my brakes. Most of our cars had a police package that included heavy duty brakes, but they would still fade once they get too hot, and I could tell they were already fading.

I pulled up to the house and found Sid on his hands and knees, crawling around in the grass. A man was lying a few feet away from him, cursing at both of us.

"You bastards!" he kept repeating.

"Sid, are you okay?"

He didn't answer my question.

What he said was, "I shot him in the leg! He threatened me with that chair," and pointed to a folding lawn chair.

I looked him over anyway, wondering why he was on his hands and knees. He was uninjured.

Then I looked at the guy.

"That bastard shot me! I'm suing all of you," he said.

I checked him for wounds and found a small hole in his thigh—like it was made with a small icepick, not a 9mm. There was no exit wound and no sign it had broken the bone. Other than some swelling, it looked almost superficial. I handcuffed him and left him lying on the grass.

Sid told me about the warrant, about losing his PR-24, and that the man had picked up the aluminum lounge chair and threatened him with it, so he shot him in the leg.

Sirens were coming from everywhere now. Sid was hyperventilating and collapsed as other officers and fire-rescue arrived. I snuck away, hoping no supervisor would show up and ask about the prisoner in the back of my car.

I knew that guy could have stood up at any time and kicked Sid's ass or disarmed him and shot him with his own gun. The next day I went to the gun shop and traded in my 9mm for a Smith & Wesson .45.

Sid worked for another year or two and quit.

The Kid I *Almost* Killed

> *Someone reading the rough draft of this memoir thought readers might be disappointed I had never killed anyone. Another friend recently asked if I had ever pointed my weapon at anyone. Two totally opposite perspectives of what officers do every day.*

One afternoon I pulled over an old Camaro for a traffic violation, something simple, and I walked up to the driver's window.

I always started off the conversation just behind the window; that's a basic officer safety technique. If the driver wanted to shoot me, he would have to turn and lean out the window to fire. Hopefully, I would see it coming and be ready for it.

The driver was a young kid, probably eighteen, and didn't speak English. With my limited Spanish, I asked him for his driver's license. He seemed okay. I saw no sign that he was any kind of a threat, so I moved forward where I could see him reach into the console between the seats for his license.

Between his seat and the console I saw the wooden grips of a handgun. He realized I had seen the gun, and he reached for it and began to pull it out. He had a full grip on his gun, and now my gun was magically in my hand, and I was already squeezing the trigger. Another ounce of pressure and the hammer would have fallen and a .45-caliber bullet would have killed him. Just as I was about to fire he dropped the gun between his feet.

He was yelling something in Spanish I didn't understand, but I pulled him out of the car and cuffed him.

The gun was a replica of a Smith & Wesson, an exact copy of the one in my hand, but it was a pellet gun, and it was empty.

A Spanish-speaking officer stopped by and talked to the kid

for me. The officer said the young man was trying to show me it was just a toy he used to scare anyone that might threaten him.

I confiscated the pellet gun and arrested the kid for driving with a suspended license.

Later that same day, and for many days after that, I thought of how close I came to killing him. I would have been exonerated, but I know myself.

I don't think I would ever have gotten over the guilt if I had pulled that trigger.

The Sea Shells

> *Typically, mentally ill patients were transported from one hospital or one treatment center to another by private ambulances. But if the patient was violent, we got the call. One night it was my turn.*

"The patient is too violent for normal transportation," the dispatcher said.

Not the best thing I wanted to hear.

So I arrived with a backup officer, and the staff greeted us and took us to the patient's room. One staff member told me the man was passive, but "If you take away his shells, he can be very violent."

I was thinking, *WTF!*

So they opened the metal door, which was like a prison cell door, and this guy was sitting on his bed. He stood and looked at me. He was like a white version of Mike Tyson. He was a few inches shorter than I, but his arms were the size of my chest. He had no neck; his shoulders and neck were so big it was hard to tell where his shoulders stopped and his head began. He was huge, muscular huge, but like Mike Tyson, he also had that look—the look boxers give each other just before the bell rings.

As I always did, I tried to take stock of my situation if things went bad. I had a backup officer, but I didn't think the two of us could physically control him, and I didn't know if the staff would help. I had my pepper spray. It was called Plus-P, a blend of tear gas and pepper plants, but it was known to fail on some psych patients and drug users. I never carried an ASP or a nightstick, but I had my Streamlight, although I didn't think it would subdue this guy. Of course, I had the last resort in the use of force, my firearm. Using the gun, though, was out of the question unless I or my partner was dying.

The man rocked back and forth on his heels and held a mesh bag to his nose. The bag was full of seashells, and like a pendant, it was attached to a leather strap around his neck.

So here goes nothing. I told him I was going to have to handcuff him. "It's the rules," I said. "Nobody can sit behind me without cuffs."

He put his hands forward, and I put the cuffs on. I couldn't cuff him behind his back; he was just too muscle-bound. In the past, I had daisy-chained two pairs of handcuffs when a single pair wouldn't work, but also the healthcare worker had said, "You want him to be able to keep the bag of shells near his face." So I cuffed him with his hands in front. He seemed pretty relaxed, and we walked him to my car.

The car had a sheet metal and Plexiglas divider separating us. Despite his size, I didn't feel he could get to me. He might be able to break out of the car, but not through the back seat.

With my backup officer following me, I transported him to the South Florida State Hospital in Broward County. During the twenty-minute ride, he told me how the smell of the shells and the salt from the ocean brought him closer to the earth to ground him to Mother Nature, and that kept him calm. His conversation was often lucid. He seemed like an intelligent guy, but then he would drift back into the Mother Nature topic.

When he was quiet, I watched him as he looked out the window with the shells under his nose. It was a bizarre ride, and I felt sorry for him. I wished I had asked more questions, like when did this all begin, was it drugs or something genetic.

> Once we got to the hospital, I walked him inside, and he thanked me for the ride. Probably one of the easiest calls I had that week.

If Only

> *We have all said it—or thought it—or maybe heard someone else say it. We see some horrible crime: the rape or murder of a child, the senseless beating of a defenseless person, and we think, just give me a few minutes alone with that guy and I'll show him some justice. Think of Jimmy Rice or Adam Walsh, those two boys' names pop up when I think of the monsters walking amongst us.*

I was dispatched along with a second officer to the station to transport a prisoner to our jail for processing. At the time, our jail was still across town at city hall. Usually, it was a one-man job, but they sent two of us.

The prisoner was a small, wimpy-looking guy, already handcuffed. I put him in the back of my car and Joe, the other officer, followed me across town. As we walked to the elevator, I read the arrest form—sexual battery. The victim was the prisoner's girlfriend's two-year-old son. I showed the arrest form to Joe as we got in the elevator and watched him read the charges. He looked up at me, and I know we were thinking the same thing. One of us stood on each side of the guy. If there was ever the perfect moment, it was then. There were no cameras, the jail was three or four floors above, and the elevator was always slow.

I fantasized about what I wanted to do to this guy. I had seen it happen in movies and on television. An officer beats the prisoner and says he fell or tripped and everybody laughs.

I enjoyed that quick fantasy, knowing Joe and I would never hit an unarmed, handcuffed creep like this guy.

We walked the guy into the Hialeah jail, where jailers took his fingerprints, his mugshots, did some paperwork, then I transported him to the Dade County Jail. The guy never spoke a single word during that long ride—he stared straight ahead like maybe he knew what was going to happen to him once he got inside the main jail.

Sexual offenders are usually placed in solitary confinement for their own safety. Other prisoners are known to beat sex offenders. I suppose it's some type of criminal code of justice.

The Big Teddy Bear

Domestic violence calls were once considered the most dangerous dispatched call for a police officer. This is a paragraph from DomesticShelters.Org.

"Domestic violence has been found to constitute the single largest category of police calls in some cities. When police officers respond, they know the situation can be volatile for both them and the abuser's victim. That's because the killer in almost one-third of all female homicides is an intimate partner, and 22 percent of officer 'line of duty' deaths in recent years occurred while responding to domestic violence calls."

So we take domestic violence calls very seriously.

One afternoon I was dispatched to a 34 domestic. The 34 was

our code for any type of disturbance. While I was on my way, the dispatcher added that a woman was being held against her will, which ramped up my expectations. I arrived with a backup officer, and we knocked on the door— I was ready for anything.

A big man opened the door just wide enough so I could see his face. I'm 5'11", and he was at least four or five inches taller. In the background, behind the door, I heard a woman crying and asking for help.

"Help me, he won't let me leave," were her exact words.

"We're just having an argument, we don't need you," he said and tried closing the door.

I stuck my boot in the opening, then he tried to slam it shut against my foot.

I body-slammed the door as hard as I could and walked past him. I think he was shocked I had used so much force. He stood there with a blank look on his face as I put myself between him and his girlfriend. I expected my backup officer to be right next to me, but he wasn't even in the room. I looked out the still-open door and saw him in the parking lot, talking on his radio.

"You have no right to be in my house," the man said.

I glanced behind me and saw a girl sobbing. She was sitting on the floor, backed into a corner.

"I just want to leave. I've been here all day, and he won't let me leave," she said.

On this call and almost every call, I had my flashlight tucked into my left armpit—even in the daylight. It's an excellent light source, and an unintimidating weapon. For me and most officers, it was the last step in the use of force before using our firearm.

The blank look on big guy's face slowly faded. Now he was mad as hell.

"You have no right to be in my house!" he repeated.

"I have every right, and I'm not leaving."

I watched as this angry giant of a man balled up his fist and prepared to throw a roundhouse punch. It was so telegraphed that it was easy to dodge. As his fist went by my face, I hit him in the head as hard as I could with the flashlight.

The sound was horrible, like a watermelon or a coconut cracking on a sidewalk. At first, I was afraid I might have killed him—but he just looked at me, and I thought, *Oh shit, all I've done is piss him off!* My backup was still outside. I was going to have to fight this monster myself.

Just as I prepared to hit him again, his eyes rolled back in his head, and he fell to the floor. I put the cuffs on him as fast as I could as the other officer walked in. I had a few words with my backup about his abrupt need to use his radio, and I left it at that.

By now, it looked like someone had implanted a golf ball under the skin of the man's forehead. I called for rescue, and when they arrived, they took one look at the huge hematoma and said they would need to transport him to the county hospital.

I sat in the ER with this guy for six hours listening to him cry about his girlfriend and listened to his never-ending apologies.

One of the nurses asked him, "Who did this to you?"

"He did," he said, pointing at me.

The nurse looked at me and said, "He's just a big teddy bear. Why did you have to hit him?"

I was embarrassed, but how would I explain something like this to a nurse? The guy now looked like a big wimp, lying there shackled to the bed, sobbing like a three-year-old.

If the case went to trial, I never received a subpoena. In fact, I don't remember ever going to any domestic violence trial. Most were thrown out when one party refused to prosecute. Those that were charged often pled to time served, and the defendant was sent to an anger management course.

My Badge

> *I was telling my friends about this call last night, about how I lost my badge, when Susan said, "I was the dispatcher that night!" I had forgotten she was involved in this call.*

One night a domestic call was dispatched to one of my zone partners. As usual, if I wasn't already on a call, I would head in their direction, just in case, and this night I was glad I did.

I was still a mile or more away when the dispatched officer screamed into her radio, 3-15!

We never liked asking for a 3-15, we reserved that signal for the times we were getting the shit kicked out of us, and by the tone of her voice, it was. Her voice was garbled, with an intelligible word now and then, like she was being punched or was on the floor fighting for her life.

The officer came on the air without using her unit number, which happens to all of us under stress. Susan recognized the officer's voice, though, and started routing other officers to her.

I flew into the parking lot with my lights and siren on and saw the officer struggling with a man in the doorway of an apartment. I took off running with another officer, Terry, right behind me. At full speed, I launched myself at the man, grabbing him in a bear hug and ripping him away from the officer. Then Terry landed on top of us. Terry is a big man and the impact must have looked spectacular, but I was struggling to get the man under me handcuffed.

Too often, a battered wife will attack the police officer

arresting her husband and this victim did just that. She and her husband were both charged with battery on a law enforcement officer.

Once we had secured them, I realized my badge and my pens had been ripped off my shirt. We looked everywhere for the badge, and I finally gave it up as being lost.

Later, as I was getting into my car to write a use-of-force report, I felt something sharp inside my bulletproof vest. After it had been ripped off, the badge had somehow slipped inside the collar of my shirt and was stuck between the vest and my T-shirt.

***

The original officer was okay. She was a tough cop but left the department a few years later in search of a new career.

The badge I was wearing that night was the original one given to me by Mayor Dale Bennett and Chief Larry Leggett. It is one of the items I retired with that I cherish the most. I still have it, now encased in Lucite.

The badge and my name tag have a few battle scars. I wish they could talk because they would have a few tales of their own.

Domestic Violence

> *While I'm on the topic, I want to mention domestic violence calls took up a good portion of our time on the road. It would not be an exaggeration to say I went to half a dozen of them every night, and they were always different.*

When there was violence, it ended quickly with an arrest. But more often than not it was just arguing, someone wanting to blow off steam, then it was up to me to mediate and defuse the situation, which I eventually became pretty good at doing.

I would often go to the same house or apartment and recognize the people as I arrived. Sometimes one of them would be beaten up, usually the wife, and the husband would be gone.

"I thought you were going to leave him," I said, all too often.

Each time I went, I saw things were worse, and I would write another report and urge the woman to press charges, but for various reasons, some never did.

Fortunately for me, none of the women I counseled were ever murdered. But I handled quite a few homicides that were the result of domestic violence, and many of them had been advised to prosecute or leave the man, but for whatever reason, they stayed with him. Some of those who did leave were tracked down by their ex and killed.

A domestic violence injunction, also known as a restraining order, is a start. It may be all that is needed for an average spouse to leave, but it is just a piece of paper to someone who's ready to commit murder.

The Vendor

For years Hialeah's intersections had been plagued by vendors walking between traffic, selling everything from peanuts, water, churros, tamales, frozen fish, and flowers. There were also window washers and people passing out advertisements and selling newspapers, and only the newspaper vendors were protected by law. On any given weekend there would be at least two dozen vendors walking in the intersection of Red Road and 49th Street, one of the busiest intersections in Hialeah.

There were complaints, mostly from motorists trying to get

through an already-crowded intersection, as some drivers would stop during a green light to buy a pound of shrimp or a bottle of water.

As a fellow motorist often stuck in these same crazy traffic jams, I sympathized with the other drivers. Sure the vendors were just trying to make a living, trying to put food on the table, but they were also taking money from local businesses, licensed businesses who paid taxes and rent and employed other people who were also paying taxes—and those taxes paid my salary.

The city gave these guys a wide berth, and one of our politicians said the country was founded on the backs of people just like them…until one of the politicians' wives bought a flower shop.

Things changed dramatically then. We had orders to run off the flower vendors and to arrest them if they refused to leave. No mention though about the churro vendors.

It was worse on Mother's Day and Valentine's Day. At roll call, sergeants were required to read orders from city hall to keep an eye out for flower vendors, chase them off, confiscate their flowers, and issue citations. Our higher-ups would drive around looking for the vendors and call for an officer to come to the scene. Often those officers would have to explain why they hadn't found the vendor first and taken the proper action. Some officers were reprimanded for failing to take action.

There were a lot of legal battles going on, too. The vendors were showing up at city hall during council meetings, demanding the right to sell their goods.

So the councilmen and women, being concerned about their voters, created a vendor's license. The vendors would have to pay an annual fee, and they would receive an itinerate vendor's license. I'm not sure how much it cost, a hundred dollars maybe, but if the city sold a thousand of them it was a win-win.

The problem was in the fine print, which said they had to keep moving and have their merchandise on them at all times, basically a license to sell door to door, not car to car in the middle of traffic. So all the vendors had was a useless license, and the battles continued, peaking each year on Mother's Day and Valentine's Day.

One day I got the call, "Flower vendor at Red and 49." So I ran the poor girl off. I also told a guy selling churros he had to leave, but he refused—so now what?

I found a Florida state statute prohibiting pedestrians from standing in the roadway for the purpose of selling merchandise to motorists, so I wrote the man a traffic ticket, and he left.

The next day he was back in the same street. I arrested him, put him in the back of my car, and filled out an arrest form. I charged him with failure to obey a lawful order and referred to the traffic statute. I released him right there when he signed a promise to appear at the bottom of the report and again, he left.

The following morning I was asleep at home when my phone rang. It was the patrol captain wanting to know where my ticket book was.

"Why, Captain?"

"The chief wants it, something about a vendor."

Holy shit.

"Captain, it's in the trunk of my car."

"Come to my office after roll call," he said.

So that afternoon I sat in the captain's office explaining what I did with the vendor and why. He asked to see my copies of the ticket and the arrest form. I thought he was going to keep them and they would eventually vanish, but he handed them back to me. He knew I had done everything right.

I left roll call and headed out to Red Road and 49th, and there was the vendor, selling his churros in traffic again. I arrested him, and this time he was going to take the long ride.

As I was filling out the arrest form, the mayor himself drove up and parked next to me. Through my open window I said, "Mayor Martinez, I've been trying to get these vendors out of the street, but this one's not cooperating."

"We didn't mean to put those people in jail," he said.

"Do you want me to let him go?" I asked.

"I don't want to interfere, officer," he said and drove away.

The vendor sat in the back of my car calling me every name he knew in English and a lot more in Spanish as we rode to the Dade County Jail.

The next day I was called into the captain's office again. This time it was a complaint from the mayor's office. My vendor got out of jail, probably thirty minutes after I dropped him off, and went straight to the mayor's office where he said I had called the mayor an "asshole."

I didn't, by the way, but I think the mayor believed the vendor.

I never bothered another vendor after that visit to the captain's office. I think I even bought a few roses from them.

***

Imagine a police officer tells someone they are doing something illegal, and they must stop, but they refuse—should the officer just shrug his shoulders and walk away? Does he ignore that person and run the others off?

This incident is very much like the incident in New York

involving Eric Garner, a vendor selling cigarettes. Departmental brass ordered officers to clear vendors competing with a local store. Eric Garner refused to leave and died a tragic death that is still unresolved.

The Teacher

One busy afternoon I had been going from call to call when the alert tone sounded. The dispatcher told me to clear the call I was on, and another officer and I were dispatched to an occupied burglary in progress.

The dispatcher said the call had been holding as a simple burglary for thirty minutes but was upgraded to in-progress when the complainant called back and said men were still inside her house.

I cleared the call I was on immediately, and other officers from all over the city and I raced to the woman's home with our lights and sirens blazing, hoping we could get there in time to save her and catch the burglars in the act.

I turned my siren off two blocks away, parked down the street, and ran to the house with my gun drawn. The other officers were doing the same thing, and we surrounded the house.

As I crept closer, a woman came out the front door and saw me with my gun in my hand and smiled. "It's okay, no one is here. I just said that because I was tired of waiting."

I took her to jail and she cried all the way.

She was an elementary school teacher and had no prior criminal history. Some people might say I used poor judgment in arresting this woman, but the way I see it, she put a lot of people at risk. The backup officers and I, all responding in emergency mode, could have easily wrecked and been injured or injured some civilian or maybe caused someone else to wreck, all because this woman didn't want to wait a few more minutes.

That night and the next day, I had several officers and two politicians call to ask me to drop the charges, and I refused. The case never went to trial, and I assume the woman pled guilty and received some type of community service.

Her adjudication of guilt was probably also withheld, meaning she would have no criminal history, which was standard practice for the state's attorney. I have no problem with that, but I hope the teacher learned a lesson, and by word of mouth it might have gotten around to a few others not to play games with the police.

The Bag Lady

Every city has at least one bag lady, and we had several. One, in particular, was a real nuisance, and she walked up and down 49th Street for most of my career. I was dispatched at least weekly on this woman, and other officers were dispatched to her every day for one reason or another. Every officer knew her.

Walking up and down the street was totally legal of course and even pushing a merchant's shopping cart off the property was usually ignored. But shoplifting and bathing nude in some homeowner's front yard was a problem.

By the time we arrived, she was usually dressed and on the move again. Most of the merchants and homeowners were forced to remove the handles of their faucets to keep her off their property.

Her crimes were always misdemeanors, and there wasn't much we could do but run her off. She was usually very quiet and seldom spoke at all. In the worst cases, officers would try to locate one of her family members, but over the years the family would hang up on the dispatchers and sometimes even curse them out. I spoke once to her son, who asked me never to call him again. He said his mother had refused all offers of help, and she just wanted to be left alone.

Many of the local fast-food restaurants felt sorry for her and fed her. She knew which ones would, and they were part of her circuit as she walked up and down the several miles of 49th.

One night, I got a call on 60th Street about a nude woman bathing in someone's yard—I was surprised at how far she was from her regular route. I found her at a Tom Thumb store. The store manager had caught her shoplifting, and I had to take her into custody.

This night she had not one, but two, shopping carts, and they were both full of her personal belongings. I couldn't just leave them there with all her things in them, so I was going to impound them: not the carts themselves, but all the stuff inside them.

The carts were full of the thin plastic shopping bags from Walmart or Publix, hundreds of them, all full of stuff. I opened the first one and found some odd pieces of mail and cash. In the first bag was ten dollars or maybe twenty, mostly in ones and fives.

The next bag was the same, and so was the next. I looked through all the bags in the carts and called for a backup officer to help me and to be a witness. I always tried to have someone with me when I dealt with a large amount of cash, just in case someone accused me later of stealing.

My fellow officer and I counted out seventeen thousand dollars in small bills on the hood of my car—and she had several bank account statements and savings books showing another twenty or thirty thousand dollars.

All those years people felt sorry for her, gave her food and money, and she was carrying around more money than some of those same people made in a year.

At the time, I worried the local crime reporter would publish my report in the *Miami Herald*, and the woman would be robbed, but it never happened.

I doubt she's still walking 49th Street; she's probably living in a big house somewhere, sitting on the porch with her feet up, sipping white wine with a smile on her face. Or maybe she's in an institution with round-the-clock supervision; either way, she's just another face and just another story in my memory bank.

Chapter 31

Drugs

Some people want to believe drug use is a victimless, non-violent crime. I know from experience that illegal drug users leave a trail of victims in their wake, including themselves. Crime and violence follow them like parasites on a dog.

Earlier, I mentioned I often profiled people.

Not long into my first year on the department, I worked in an area called Seminola, a historically black neighborhood in Hialeah. At the time, it was *the* place to go for crack cocaine.

White and Hispanic people drove into the all-black neighborhood looking for illegal drugs. Those white faces stood out like sore thumbs as they circled two small grocery stores, Kitchen's and Johnson's, in search of the sellers standing in the shadows. It was like shooting fish in a barrel.

I made hundreds of drug arrests in my career; sometimes several in a single night, and out of all those hundreds, there are three people who stick out in my mind when I think of drug addiction. The first one is Jackie.

Jackie Hernandez

One night I watched a white guy through my binoculars as he circled through Seminola looking for crack cocaine. I arrested him and his passenger after he bought a single five-dollar rock.

The man was in his late 50s, and his passenger was Jackie Hernandez; she was young, around eighteen, and an attractive woman.

It was obvious to me what was going on, but I let her tell me anyway.

"He bought me a rock, and I was going to give him a blow job." She confided in me that she had been smoking crack for several months and was so addicted she had resorted to prostitution to pay for it.

I looked at this attractive eighteen-year-old young woman and imagined how desperate she must have been to be giving that old man a blow job in the front seat of his car. She traded those first few minutes of euphoria for her dignity, then she would start all over again.

I took her to jail that night, and many nights after that.

Jackie was always polite and seemed like an intelligent woman. I ran into her often, sometimes every other day. Over the years I watched crack take its toll on her. By the time she was thirty, she looked like an anorexic, sixty-year-old hag.

Then there was a gap that lasted six months, and one day on a call, a woman walked up to me and said, "Sergeant Shaw!"

I didn't recognize her.

"It's me, Jackie!"

She looked like a different person, like the Jackie I remembered years ago. She told me she had spent the last several months in rehab and now lived with a relative. She said she was clean, and she looked healthy and happy. I was happy for her, too. At the time, she was the first person I had seen beat the crack addiction.

It didn't last long, though, and once again, I found her in Seminola, back to her old tricks. Over the remaining years, she withered away again.

Not long before I was transferred to homicide, I was patrolling along Palm Avenue when I saw someone sleeping in a planter—yes, a planter. I stopped and saw what I thought was an old woman curled up around a palm tree, and she was barely conscious. I called for fire-rescue, and it wasn't until they arrived and began working on her that I realized it was Jackie.

She was bone-thin, missing most of her teeth, and had open sores all over her face and arms.

Rescue knew her, too. "She's dying from AIDS," they said.

Not long after, I heard she had passed away.

She was 40 years old.

Adonis

> *I called this kid Adonis, which wasn't his real name, but he looked like a male model or like the Greek god Adonis, only with dark hair.*

One night I saw a white face behind the wheel of a beat-up old Chevrolet Impala driving slowly past Kitchen's in Seminola, where the crack sellers hung out. I couldn't catch the sellers; they would run and get inside a house faster than I could get out of my car. The narcotics guys took care of the sellers—I took care of the buyers.

I fell in behind the car, and it took off, racing down the street for several blocks. The driver eventually lost control, crashed, and gave up. I arrested him for fleeing and eluding an officer. I searched his car pursuant to arrest (I always used that term because it gave me the right to search) and discovered the trunk was full of stereo and electronic appliances.

One of the officers helping me had just handled a burglary, and all the stuff in the trunk matched what was stolen. Sure enough, it was from the burglary, and my driver admitted to the crime. He was sent off to jail, his car was towed to the pound, and the burglary victim got all his stuff back. Sweet!

Maybe a month later I saw the same car driving in a different area of town. It was daylight, and I decided to follow him. While I was following him, I had the dispatcher run the license plate and a driver's license check on the owner. It was the same guy, and his license was now suspended.

I popped the blue lights and off he goes again for several blocks. Drugs must have messed up his mind because he pulled into an almost-vacant parking lot, jumped out of his car, and ran.

I wondered about his sanity because I had no need to get out of my car. It was a big, open parking lot, and I drove right behind him knowing he was going to tire out long before my car did. But I got too close and one of his heels hit my bumper, and he fell. I couldn't stop in time, and I ran over him.

I thought I might have just killed the guy, then I heard thumping sounds from under the floorboards and opened my door to check. As I did, he came out from under the car and took off running again.

As I ran after him, I lost him between a row of parked cars, but in the window of one apartment, a woman looked at me, pointed to the ground in front of her, and I walked up with my .45 out and ready.

He had nowhere to go but right at me, and he did.

They don't encourage this in the academy, but I smashed him

in the side of the head with my gun, and he went down. I didn't plan to use the gun as a club, but it was all I had.

I cuffed him and looked him over. He had a small hematoma over his ear from the gun along with burns and scrapes all over from being under the car, but nothing serious. I took him downtown again.

For the next several days my thumb ached, and I wondered if it was broken. Somehow it had gotten caught between the gun's slide and the side of the guy's head.

I saw this same guy on and off over most of my career, and like Jackie, he looked worse every time. I arrested him several more times over the next few years, then he vanished. I don't know what happened to him. Hopefully, he got clean, but I doubt it.

Not long ago I forwarded this memory to a friend and former coworker. He thinks the guy's name was Manny, and if it was the same guy, Manny also died from AIDS.

***

This was a known felon fleeing from law enforcement. I couldn't shoot him, but I wasn't going to let him get away, either. Today I consider myself lucky. A video of me hitting a subject in the side of the head with my firearm could end up in the news. But this was the nineties, and fortunately today's smartphones hadn't been invented yet. I mention this not because I am proud of it, but because it was part of this memory.

To this day there is only one person I know who has beaten cocaine addiction.

The Family

In all the years I went to this house, I never met the woman's son. I was called to her home at least a dozen times over twenty years, and I imagine other officers went to the house just as often. It was on the corner across the street from my junior high school, so it was easy to remember.

The call was some type of family problem, a domestic, just a mother and father wanting advice about their troubled son, one of the thousands of similar calls. Then there was the second call. This second call might have been just as benign, but the parents were more desperate for help.

Their son was in high school now, and they caught him stealing money from them. The mom didn't want to press charges—she didn't even want a police report, and I saw the tension between her and her husband. As usual, I urged them to get civil help. We had brochures with all types of information about dealing with domestic, psychological, and drug issues. If they ever read those brochures, they never took any action.

There was often a younger daughter in the house as well, but the parents never called the police while the son was home. I think the mother waited for him to leave.

One day I was sent to the house to take a report of a stolen car. Only the mom was home that day, and she told me her now-adult son had taken the family car to a salvage yard and had it crushed for drug money. She still didn't want to prosecute, she was again hoping I had the answer that would turn her son around and restore her family. I wrote her an information report and handed her another case number and my card.

The next time, the television and stereo system were gone.

She told me the stress involving her son had ended her marriage and even her daughter had moved away.

The last time I went the woman greeted me in an almost-empty living room. The son had taken most of the furniture. She looked horrible—like she had aged twenty years in just the last few months. She had given up on her own life, but not on her son.

That was the last time I was dispatched to this house.

***

A note for civilians: there are two options available to a family in this situation. One is the Baker Act. This allows an officer to take a person into custody, against their will, for a psychiatric evaluation lasting no more than three days. But the officer must have seen and be able to articulate that the person is an imminent threat to himself or to others. I was never able to Baker Act this guy.

The other option is an ex parte: an order from a judge that authorizes an officer to take a person into custody for medical or psychiatric treatment. The family does all the legwork on an ex parte. It's not easy, and it's not free.

CHAPTER 32

REALLY RANDOM EVENTS

What's Mundane?

I think back to some of the mundane calls I handled every day, the tens of thousands that were so insignificant they are lost forever, the countless domestic disputes or the endless number of shoplifters I had to arrest. But I know that to the average person, those calls are anything but mundane.

After instructing at the academy, I went back to patrol and worked as a field training officer, teaching new officers what we did, what we didn't do, what to look for, and most importantly, how to survive and go home at the end of the shift in one piece. I suppose my time as an instructor gave my supervisors the idea of using me as an officer in the Ride-Along program.

This program offered members of the community the chance to ride in a police car and to witness firsthand what we do. I was the lucky officer most sergeants picked. I'm being sarcastic of course, having some unknown person in my car as I was patrolling and handling calls was often a distraction. I had to worry not just about my life but that of someone who had no police training at all. And I had to make sure everything I said and did looked professional. It wasn't as easy as it sounds.

One night they assigned a young Hispanic reporter from a local news station to ride with me. She seemed nice, and things went well for the first few hours until the sun went down.

When the sun sets and it's dark outside, perspective changes. After all, we weren't driving to the mall to shop or to a restaurant for dinner. We were looking for crime. We were looking for evil people doing bad things. I knew it, and I think this poor reporter was feeling it then, too.

Soon we were dispatched on our first domestic dispute. It was a typical argument between a husband and his wife, an easy call, no sign of violence, and both the man and the woman were calm. For me, it was all very forgettable.

But the reporter was terrified. I had asked her to translate something, and she could barely speak. She was physically trembling, and her face was pale when we got back to the car. This lasted for hours and finally she said, "I've seen enough, take me back."

To the average citizen, what we do is anything but mundane.

***

Reading the stories above may give the impression I would have wanted less violence, less gore, less danger, but that would be wrong. Many officers, including me, worked as much overtime as we could. The money was great, but the real reason was the adrenaline rush. It was like an addiction for us. I often worked all three of my days off, and at least once a week I worked a double shift. A night without something sensational was frustrating, and the long hours of silence on the radio during a midnight shift were painful, but I knew, at any moment, some officer could come on the radio screaming for help. There would be a burglary in progress or a foot chase or even a homicide, and we lived for those moments.

The Wheelchair

One afternoon I arrested a man in a wheelchair. This wasn't a victim of old age or a traffic accident, this was a twenty-one-year-old gang member who had been shot and paralyzed by a rival thug. Before he was paralyzed, he was known in our city as extremely violent, and being in a wheelchair didn't change his personality.

He had beaten his mother this time, and I charged him with domestic battery. Even sitting in the wheelchair he fought as I tried to handcuff him. I had to dump him out of the chair and onto the grass of his front yard. Tucked inside his wheelchair was a .38-caliber revolver. It took two of us to handcuff him and get him inside my patrol car.

I had communications call the jail and the corrections officers met me outside and helped me get him out of the car and inside. I never saw or heard of that man again.

I was lucky that day. I was so focused on the optics of struggling with a disabled man I never thought of searching him first. It could have been a fatal mistake on my part. I can picture that scene happening today—a video playing out on CNN all day for a week as two brutal cops struggled with a paraplegic man in a wheelchair.

The One-Armed Guy

I also arrested a one-armed violent drunk one night. How did I handcuff a one-armed man? Easy—I ran the other cuff through and around his belt.

Granny

Embarrassingly enough, I also arrested a seventy-year-old grandmother for shoplifting. This grandmother had stolen something at K-Mart valued over $100. At that time, a hundred dollars was the threshold for a felony, and the store security officer had the arrest form completed and waiting for me when I arrived. I asked her if the arrest was necessary—couldn't she just call a family member or anything other than making me transport this old woman? But the security officer was adamant, and I had no choice. It was a felony, and she wanted to prosecute.

To make matters worse, the woman was refusing to cooperate. I wanted to let her sign the promise to appear affidavit in our jail, but she refused. Technically, the affidavit was only used for misdemeanors, but so what, I thought. So this woman, someone's elderly grandmother I'm sure, took the long ride to the Women's Annex of the Dade County Jail.

I walked her in and I felt like an ass. The look in the jailer's eyes made me want to explain what had happened, but none of the words seemed right. Here I was, putting this petite, elderly woman in a jail full of prostitutes and drug addicts.

I never liked that store security officer, but I had to deal with her for the next several years.

Chapter 33

SWAT

I wish I had a handful of exciting stories to tell about SWAT, but most, if not all, of them were mundane, ordinary, or boring. I was in SWAT for two years, and during those years I was called out maybe a dozen times.

SWAT in Hialeah was just beginning to be a professional unit. The city was finally giving us a real budget and real training. SWAT school was three weeks long and held at the Metro-Dade training grounds. During those weeks we fired thousands and thousands of rounds out of every type weapon available. Just hitting a target wasn't enough: in SWAT we had to be able to hit the X in the 10 ring, about a two-inch circle, every time.

We learned to rappel out of three-story buildings, how to tie knots in the ropes that would save our lives, shoot while wearing a gas mask in a cloud of tear gas, and finally, how to work as a team.

For me, the experience and the education I gained from this school were more rewarding than actually putting them to use. I achieved a sense of expertise, a feeling of proficiency, and falsely, a sense of invulnerability that remained with me for the rest of my career.

After we graduated we continued to train twice a month. One day we would be at the firing range and the other we would practice entering different types of building, using the tools to pry open a door or to smash it in, then clearing the inside and securing "prisoners." A SWAT entry is fine-tuned and choreographed, and everyone had an assigned position.

We cross-trained often, in case of an emergency. We had two teams, and my position on one of those teams was lead penetrator. I know it sounds bad, but I was just the first man through the door. All I carried was my pistol, but I wore a heavy ceramic vest that covered my chest, back, and thighs. It was an inch thick and weighed eighty or ninety pounds and was supposed to be capable of stopping a bullet from a high-powered rifle.

As a penetrator, my job was to get to the target as fast as possible. Sometimes the target was a wanted person; sometimes it was narcotics. The second penetrator, my partner going through the door, literally had my back. He usually clung to my vest, and his job was to keep me safe as I rushed in and to engage anyone trying to stop me. More people followed us, with long guns like assault rifles and shotguns, and they would break off and secure anyone inside. Most entries were over in seconds. The preparations for entry, however, would often take hours.

The few entries I made were narcotic raids, and no one ever resisted or got in our way. Those raids weren't much different, or more exciting, than our training raids. Most of the people I passed in the hallways of their own homes were frozen in fear and never resisted. After each of the callouts, I hoped that the next one would be the exciting one, like the ones on TV or in a Hollywood movie.

There were a few SWAT calls where I was on an outside

perimeter while the second team of penetrators did the entry. Our job then was to grab anyone running out the back door.

Those were the standard or typical callouts. But there were others.

One night we were called out when an informant told us his gang was planning a home invasion in a rural section of Hialeah. They were supposedly heavily armed, and several of us hid inside the home, and a few more formed a perimeter outside in the thickly wooded fields. We were getting updates from the informant as they got closer and closer, and the adrenaline rushes after each update were tremendous.

In the end, a couple of guys got out of a car in the driveway and were taken down by the perimeter team. It was a disappointment.

***

This next call had us all pumped up, too. This one was going to be the big one, I thought. This one was serious, or so we all hoped.

For several months in 1986, two men named William Matix and Michael Platt were on a three-month crime spree of murder, bank robberies, and armored car hijackings all over Dade County. They were heavily armed with assault rifles, shotguns, and handguns.

Our department got a tip they were going to rob one of two different banks in Hialeah, and we had two days to prepare.

We commandeered two of the city's trash trucks that had steel siding, and we practiced pulling up in the big truck and engaging the men in the parking lot. We hoped the steel was thick enough to stop a high-powered rifle.

That day came, and we all felt ready. We were confident—we

wanted to engage these men and kill them if necessary. We sat, in full SWAT gear in South Florida's heat, in the back of that truck for hours until we heard they had been engaged by the FBI several miles away.

After a horrible shootout, two FBI agents and both gunmen were dead, five other agents were seriously wounded, and more than 125 rounds were fired. Maybe we were lucky that day and the FBI wasn't; maybe we all would have been killed.

Google the names of these killers to read the entire horrible backstory and to understand what I mean by being lucky.

Two years of training wearing that heavy vest and jumping out of that big SWAT van twenty times a day finally took its toll on my knees and I had to quit.

***

I was promoted to sergeant soon after leaving SWAT and went on to become the city's hostage negotiations sergeant. Training began at Metro-Dade's Hostage Negotiations School. For two weeks I learned how to negotiate with persons suffering from different types of mental illnesses or those taking hostages in the middle of a violent crime.

I supervised eight other negotiators. We were called out a few dozen times, mostly people holding themselves hostage, threatening to kill themselves for various reasons. We never had any of those exciting scenes I see in movies. Ours were often boring, and the negotiations frequently dragged on for hours and hours, but we never lost anyone.

After two years, one of the other negotiators was promoted to sergeant, and I felt I was ready to move on, leaving him in control of the unit. I used those negotiating skills for the remainder of my career and still find them useful today.

CHAPTER 34

THE DOG

This story is not a pleasant story for dog lovers. I've always liked dogs and loved my own, so I know.

In my career, I fired approximately one hundred thousand rounds of ammunition in practice. This is not my estimate, but one a friend of mine came up with. I asked him once, "Ed, you know everything I've done during my career, how many rounds do you think I fired—ten thousand, twenty thousand?"

He did the math and called me the next day. "I think one hundred thousand, give or take a few."

The number seemed shockingly high at first. But I thought about it.

An officer shoots a lot of ammunition just in the academy, then there are annual qualifications, add SWAT school, then twice-monthly SWAT training with sniper rifles, shotguns, assault rifles, and pistols. I was also a firearms training instructor, and during that certification, I fired another couple of thousand rounds. I was on the city's short-lived combat pistol team, and I competed in three Police Olympics. I shot a thousand rounds a week during some of those years.

After thousands of rounds fired during practice—I fired a total of four rounds on the street. This story is about two of them.

In 1990, I was on patrol and dispatched to a disturbance call. A man had been bitten by his neighbor's dog. As I parked my patrol car, I saw a woman standing next door, pointing to the backyard of her neighbor's house. There were no sounds or warnings that prepared me for what I was about to see.

I walked around the corner of the house, and I saw a huge dog about ten feet in front of me. At first, I thought it was a Great Dane. Making it look even bigger, it had a small dog, a Pekinese, in its mouth. Both dogs were motionless. The big dog looked like it was standing at attention—like a statue in a museum, facing me head-on. Then I noticed the little dog move one of its legs, so I knew it was still alive.

To my left was an old man leaning against a chain-link fence. The woman I saw in the front yard was now behind him on the other side of the fence. The man was holding his wrist; his forearm was covered in blood and tissue—actually muscle and tendons—which had been ripped free from the bone and now hung below his fingers. A thick stream of blood was flowing onto the grass at his feet. The man never said a word. He was in shock. His skin was pasty white, and he looked like he was about to pass out. It was his Pekinese in the big dog's mouth.

As usual, I don't remember taking my gun out of the holster, but it was already pointed at the motionless big dog.

"Kill it!" the woman yelled. "Shoot it!"

The adrenaline rush had begun. I may have already described its effects, but I'll repeat them. Time slowed, yet my brain ran at lightning speed as I tried to take in everything I saw and heard—too focused to be aware of emotions.

"Kill it!" The woman repeated.

I had both tunnel vision and a wide-angle view of everything around me; how both are possible, I don't know.

Several conflicting thoughts were running through my head–-if I shot the big dog, I could miss and kill the little dog—and I would be blamed for its death. The big dog wasn't a deadly threat to me, at least not yet. I looked past the dog at the house behind it, and I didn't see anyone outside. Still, there were windows, and if I missed the dog, I might hit someone in the house.

Other thoughts on my list were, What will internal affairs say? What will my chief say?

"Kill it! Kill it!"

I was in a staring contest with this big dog and I needed to act.

At my feet were several lengths of white PVC pipe. With my left hand, I picked up the longest one, which was about eight feet long, while still aiming my .45 at the dog with my right hand. My plan was to whack the dog with the pipe; hopefully, he would drop the Pekinese and run away—it would be a win-win.

What happened next was a blur. As I was about to hit the dog, it dropped the little one and leaped—with a deep, loud growling roar and huge teeth bared, it was in mid-air, coming right at me.

My gun fired. I saw the bullet hit the dog just below the neck on the left side of its chest. A little red spot appeared on its fur, followed by a big pink spray of blood coming out its left side where the bullet had exited. The dog seemed to spin in mid-air.

When it landed, still alive, it was facing the opposite direction, and my gun fired the second round. My years of training were running this scene now, and I watched as that last bullet took off one of its front legs. Not completely, though—it hung from its shoulder by some piece of flesh or a tendon and dangled uselessly as it ran.

Two rounds—the double tap, it's called. Fire twice and

evaluate. In SWAT I was trained to fire three times: two to the center of mass and one to the head.

Looking back, I didn't think it was possible a .45-caliber bullet would spin a 130-pound dog around. Things like that happen in the movies, but it doesn't happen in real life. The body just drops.

The dog was now running on three legs, and it was still remarkably fast. It tried to jump the fence but crashed headlong into it instead. It reversed course and ran for the front yard as my backup officer was running toward the sound of gunfire. The dog and the officer almost collided.

I couldn't see around the corner of the house, but there was more gunfire. I ran to the front yard, and found the dog was dead, collapsed against the fence.

The Pekinese was taken to an animal hospital but died.

Administration gave me the rest of the night off, a cooling-off period I guess, and that night I watched the story on the 11 o'clock news. A video showed the man arriving at the hospital with fire-rescue, and the news anchor said doctors were optimistic they could save his arm.

The big dog was an Akita mix and had jumped the fence and attacked the man's Pekinese. The owner of the Akita was arrested for bench warrants and fined for animal abuse because several more dogs and a monkey were found in cages in the backyard, and most of them were suffering from malnutrition.

It was difficult to sleep the next few nights. Internal affairs investigated every officer-involved shooting, and I worried they would find me negligent somehow. Maybe I should have done something different. I thought of the detectives and the lieutenant working in IA at the time, and the image wasn't encouraging.

All types of scenarios ran through my head, but I couldn't think of any other way I could have avoided killing the dog.

I still have nightmares about this call. The dog in mid-air, the teeth bared—in some dreams, my gun jams and the dog wins, other times I'm fired for incompetence just days before my retirement.

For weeks and months I thought if killing a dog could be this traumatic, what would it be like to shoot a human being?

Not long after this shooting, I would find out.

Chapter 35

The Next Two Rounds

It was summer, a hot night, and it was about ten o'clock. I knew because the midnight shift started at ten and soon those officers would be flooding onto my scene. The call started off with our dispatcher sending officers to a 29, a robbery in the southeastern end of the city on our border with Miami. Unfortunately for us, it was a common call in Hialeah.

I was in my patrol car waiting for a traffic light to change in the north end of the city when the alert tone sounded: *beeeep!* The *eeee* was longer than normal. Some dispatchers, either on purpose or just as a result of their own adrenaline rush, hold the alert longer.

"All units, 29 armed just occurred."

Interesting call, I thought—but too far away.

"Be advised, two elderly women were pistol-whipped and fire-rescue is en route. The subjects were two black males who fled in an early 1980s maroon two-door Chevrolet Caprice."

I was angry I wasn't closer to this call. The shortest, most logical route of escape for them would be to drive eastbound, and they would be out of our jurisdiction and back into a black neighborhood in just a few short blocks.

I was six or seven miles north of the crime in a predominantly white section of Dade County.

Three or four minutes later I watched as a 1980s maroon Caprice drove through my headlights. The driver was a black male. There was no way he hadn't seen me, so I fell in right behind him.

I picked up the microphone and said, "2241, I'm following a 1980s maroon Caprice, black male driver, northbound on West 12th Avenue."

My closest backup officer was a sergeant coming from the opposite direction a half mile away.

All communications on the radio stopped. Everyone was holding their breath hoping I had the right car. I still had doubts, though.

The Caprice continued northbound, and the driver was trying to blend in with other traffic, matching their speeds and hoping I wasn't following him. Soon we both stopped at a red light, and I was right behind him. His bumper was about two feet away from mine.

My backup officer's voice came on the radio. "2204, I'm at the red light and Shaw is right in front of me. When the light turns green have him stop the car when he's ready."

I could see the sergeant across the intersection and as the light turned green, I hit the blue lights, and the Caprice's driver floored it, making a hard right turn and disappearing into a cloud of smoke and dust.

A wild chase ensued, lasting several minutes. It was soon clear the driver was lost. He made right turns and left turns as fast as the Caprice would go, and I knew he had no clue how to get out of our city. Eventually, he made a wrong turn down a dead-end street—and I knew I had him.

Whatever was going to happen, it was going to happen right then.

This street ended in a cul-de-sac with six-foot concrete-block privacy walls on both sides. In the grass swale between the street and the walls were big coral rocks, each about a foot in diameter, that were spaced evenly every ten or fifteen feet to keep residents from parking on the grass.

The driver realized he was trapped and was going to try a U-turn, but he hit the wall, bounced off, and ended up on top of one of those big rocks. He was stuck; the car was teetering back and forth on the rock, and each time the rear wheel touched down, the car jerked forward a few inches.

That weird sensation of time slowing was starting, and I was fighting tunnel vision. I knew that my backup officer was somewhere beside me, but I needed to stay focused on the car in front of me. Nothing behind me was going to kill me; everything I needed to worry about was right inside that teetering car.

This street was dark. If there were street lights, they weren't working, and only our headlights were illuminating the Caprice. We were now surrounded by a haze of smoke from both the car's exhaust and the tire spinning every time it touched the ground. Our blue emergency lights were acting like strobes, giving the scene a weird, pulsing blue effect.

Once it was clear to me the car was stuck, I opened my door and stood behind it, using it as a cover and I had my .45 out, waiting to see what happened next. Then the driver's door opened. It was damaged and wouldn't fully open with the wall so close.

I watched the driver trying to edge his way out of the narrow opening. In his hands, I saw a huge shiny revolver, and I yelled "gun" as loud as I could, then framed the man in my gun's sights and I began squeezing the trigger.

My backup was to my right, although I still couldn't see him, but I could see the front end of his car in my peripheral vision. He had stopped at an angle, giving him a view of the passenger door.

The driver finally looked up and saw me just as my gun was about to fire, but he was unable to raise his gun because his elbows were jammed in the door. I was milliseconds from firing when the man dived back inside the car. Through the tinted rear glass, I saw his silhouette moving toward the passenger door, and I kept that silhouette in my sights.

Then the passenger door opened.

I heard the crack of a gunshot. It was loud and seemed to be directed toward me or my backup. I squeezed my trigger, and the gun fired and fired again.

I looked for movement in the Caprice, and saw nothing. I knew I had just killed those two men because I never missed.

I looked over at the sergeant and saw that he was okay. He was standing in the crook of his open door, just like I was, holding his AR-15 on the Caprice.

The air was calm; everything was deadly calm. The smoke from my gun hung in the humid air in front of me, illuminated by the pulsing blue emergency lights.

Then time sped up, and everything returned to normal. That weird sense of slowed time only lasted a second or two, then all my other senses kicked into overdrive. First, I realized I had never turned off my siren. I was standing a foot from the speaker, and I couldn't hear it. Then it was all I could hear!

I leaned into my car and turned the siren off, and grabbed my radio while still watching the Caprice for movement.

"2241, shots fired, I need fire-rescue."

I was sure the dispatcher acknowledged me, but I was so focused on the Caprice I couldn't hear her.

The sergeant covered me, and we made our way to the car to see the aftermath. We never spoke; there was no need. We were in officer survival mode and years of training and experience dictated every move.

The passenger door of the Caprice was still open. My flashlight under my arm lit up the car's interior and I saw the two men lying on the front seat, one on top of the other. As I stared at them with my gun's sights trained on the back of the driver's head, I saw the passenger was faceup, lying on his back. His eyes were wide-open, watching me, and he was terrified.

Two handguns were on the floorboard, next to the passenger's hands. With the sergeant still covering me I pulled the lifeless driver out of the car by the back of his shirt and cuffed him, then did the same with the passenger. I frisked both men, expecting to find blood on the driver, but there were no wounds of any kind—this tough guy, who had pistol-whipped two elderly women—had fainted and was uninjured. With the subjects now in handcuffs, I canceled fire-rescue, feeling foolish.

The officer handling the original robbery showed up with the victims, who were probably in their 70s. One of the women had a bandage the size of a turban on her head; they were frail and scared, but they had the courage to identify the subjects, and I'm sure it was hard for them.

In the back seat of the Caprice, we found the victims' purses. The shiny gun the driver had held earlier was a fully loaded .357 Magnum and the other, a cheap .25-caliber automatic with a single bullet in the chamber and one more in the magazine.

I knew administration would pull me off the scene soon, so one of the last things I did was look for the bullet holes in the car. I had aimed through the rear window and into the front seat where I envisioned the armed driver to be. I found my two bullet holes in the sheet metal about an inch apart and one inch below the glass. Both bullets had penetrated the first layers of sheet metal, separating the trunk from the interior, and stopped. They had mushroomed and fragmented like they're designed to do.

I remembered feeling fine; better than fine, I felt euphoric. I had just engaged two armed criminals and won. I had fired that shot, the one I always worried about, without hesitation.

Had I killed one of those men it might have been a different story. But the adrenaline was still pumping, and I felt like I needed to tell everyone what had happened, what I had seen and why I had fired—and I felt like I needed to stay busy—the very last thing I wanted to do was to go home and relax.

Soon I was led away from the scene by my friends and supervisors, a standard protocol after a shooting. Get the officer away from the chaos and make sure he's okay. Once they were sure I was mentally able to drive, they sent me home.

I didn't sleep much for a week. Every time I closed my eyes, the events played out again and again, like a movie that keeps rewinding and starting over, not the chase but the actual shooting part. Each time it replayed, I recalled something new and with better clarity than when it happened. Small things, like my blue emergency light creating a strobe effect on my rear sights and not being able to see my front sights at all. The driver's elbows pinned between his door and the wall.

This is why officers don't give a sworn statement the first day or two after a traumatic event. Prosecutors should probably do the same for witnesses because if they change or add to their statement, anything they say later sounds like a lie in court.

A few months after the shooting I was subpoenaed to court and was surprised to see the driver enter the courtroom in a wheelchair. He was paralyzed below the waist, the result of a fight in prison.

In court, the prosecutor held up the defendants' rap sheets, which were twenty pages long, and I feared they would eventually be released as they had been time and time again.

Neither man would make eye contact with me, or with their victims. I tried to get their attention. I wanted to get that last little dig in—I won, and they lost. I got the impression that they just didn't give a shit what happened. Like automatons going through the motions, it was just another day in the life of a thug.

I heard those words—life in prison, and I wanted to believe life means life, but I knew better. Years later, one of these men was killed in prison, so I guess he served his full sentence.

I had often worked side by side with officers who had killed someone. They never spoke about it, and I never asked. I didn't want to know the details, but I had always wondered what they had thought about in those few seconds before they pulled the trigger. I had needed to know, when the time came, would I be able to fire?

I'll be honest; it was a simple thing to pull the trigger. I never thought about how I was killing someone, or I was about to take another man's life. I was, in fact, stopping death. I was going to stop this man from killing my partner, or me.

Unlike the afternoon I killed the dog, this event—the squeezing of the trigger while aiming at another human being—was a choice. My partner and I were under fire, and I was going to stop it.

It wasn't until hours later I felt fear, and it was the fear of failure. If I had let those two armed robbers escape, they would have eventually killed some other victim an hour or days later, and those deaths would have haunted me.

For ten years I had wondered—would I freeze, would I hesitate, or would I fire?

Now I knew.

***

Almost twenty years later, I'm still angry—angry at the men who felt they had to prey on two old women, and angry at myself for having missed when I fired at those two thugs. All those thousands and thousands of rounds I fired in practice—and I missed. I also wonder how different things would have been if I had killed one or both of those men. Would there still be anger or would I feel remorse or guilt?

Jessie Norman, our physical training instructor, took this picture of me outside the training building just after the 1986 Florida Police Olympics. The gold medal was for the combat pistol event. So when I say I never miss, well, I guess it's not always true. As a side note, in training they say it's common to shoot low in low-light conditions; so that's my excuse.

The three silver medals were for the pentathlon, three mile cross-county run, and the 100-meter hurdles. The bronze medal was for the long jump.

Chapter 36

The Promotion to Sergeant

After some frustrating years, in 1991 I was finally promoted to sergeant. The frustrations are detailed in a later chapter, "The Gringo Lawsuit."

As a newly promoted sergeant, I was transferred to communications and spent two years as the desk sergeant, supervising civilian employees. Being assigned to communications had been used as a means of punishment by the administration, for me, it was a lack of seniority.

It was a frustrating assignment for anyone wanting to be out on the streets mixing it up with the bad guys. But it was rewarding, too. I got to experience what happens on the other end of the radio, to hear the emotions of callers and victims, and to see the dedication and professionalism of the call takers and dispatchers.

Those two years seemed like an eternity, but eventually, new promotions meant I had junior sergeants, and I went back to the midnight shift as a patrol sergeant, supervising police officers for the first time. For twelve years I had worked for dozens of sergeants, some good and some great, and now I hoped to emulate the great ones. A challenging prospect and one I took seriously.

And the deaths and tragedies— the fodder of nightmares resumed.

Chapter 37

The Quinceañera

The Quinceañera, or Quince, is the Spanish celebration of a fifteen-year-old girl's passage from childhood to womanhood.

One evening a 3-30, shots fired with injuries, was dispatched in my zone. I was the zone's sergeant, and I took the call.

It was a high-density, blue-collar neighborhood made up of townhomes and apartment buildings, and as I pulled into the parking lot, I found about twenty or thirty angry, upset teenagers outside. This neighborhood had several active gangs and most of these kids looked the type: baggy drooping pants, gang signs tattooed on their arms and chest, and their visible hatred for me—an officer in uniform.

These kids were all in their late teens, they were verbally aggressive, or pissed-off may be a better description. They were yelling at me, both in English and in Spanish, and it was impossible for me to understand what they were saying.

Alone, I looked for guns and knives, but other than their abusive attitude, found nothing threatening. Out of the corner of my eye, I saw six or seven people down, and I ran over to them.

When I say down, I mean lying down—as in wounded. Half the

crowd of teenagers were angry I wasn't chasing down the gunman who had apparently just fled, and the other half were begging me to help the injured. I was frustrated at not being able to get a description of the subjects for my officers who were on their way to the scene.

I told dispatch what I could, and I started checking the victims. Most of them had minor wounds, indicative of a small-caliber handgun, a .22 revolver perhaps, as there were no shell casings left behind I would have expected to see from a semi-automatic.

One man was worse than the others. He was the father of the young Quince girl and the host of the party. He had been shot in the mouth. The bullet had blown out a few of his teeth and shredded his tongue so he couldn't speak clearly.

I knelt over him, trying to understand what he was saying, when someone hit me from behind. Not real hard, but hard enough and I turned around. Three or four kids were behind me; they were angry and demanded I go after the shooter, who I knew was long gone. These kids were now a serious threat, and I couldn't turn my back on them.

Knowing that any of them could be armed, I pulled my .45 and stepped away from the victim. I told the dispatcher I needed an emergency backup, a 3-15, and instantly I heard sirens coming.

With my gun in my hand and the father bleeding out at my feet, the kids backed off, and in seconds, I was surrounded by other officers.

Our investigation revealed a neighboring gang had tried to crash this quince party, and the father had attempted to throw them out. Someone in the rival gang had opened fire on the crowd then, like cowards, they fled.

The father lived, and the case was turned over to detectives. I never heard if any arrests were made.

***

There were a few things I heard on the radio that both frightened and excited me.

When an officer asked for a 15, which was simply asking for a second officer or for a backup officer, I could tell by the sound of their voice if they were in trouble, or just needed advice.

Asking for a 3-15, however, was reserved for the times when the shit had hit the fan or was about to; officers didn't toy with the signal and use it indiscriminately; it was exclusively for when they were in trouble.

Although this case was similar to the one at the Sayonara Bar, the effect on me was much different. That shooting happened during my first few months out of the academy, and by this time, I had almost twenty years of experience. I had seen so many shootings, so many homicides, and been through so many stressful events, the stress at this scene seemed routine.

I was dating Susan at the time, and she was in communications, probably listening to all this, and I was worried she was freaking out. I know we talked about it later when I got home. She told me then, and still tells me, she always feared I was too aggressive or not careful enough when I was dealing with gang members. I was careful, and I felt I was always ready, but maybe I was just lucky all those years.

I was more worried about Susan hearing me ask for that 3-15 than being shot.

Chapter 38

The Right Place #2

Sometimes you're just in the right place at the right time.

Some nights I would lie in bed thinking of the events I thought were worth writing about, and this one always seemed to be out in front. It's not gory or horrific like the others; it doesn't involve death or tragedy, but for a long time it left me confused, and I found it so difficult to talk about I rarely mentioned it.

Not every call ended up giving me nightmares, but I do dream about this one. It was the first call I wrote about when I decided to write Who I Am.

I was a patrol sergeant working day shift, and if I had to work weekends, the mornings were great. I usually ate breakfast at Ranch House, then parked somewhere and did the *Miami Herald*'s crossword. It was often quiet until at least noon, when things began to change. People began getting on each other's nerves, the alcoholics began waking up, neighbors began arguing, husbands began beating their wives, cars began colliding, and I was busy for the rest of the shift.

This was a typical weekend morning, and I was sitting in my car when the alert tone sounded.

A small child was drowning in a lake, and I was literally right down the street. *A child drowning!* I slammed the car into gear and hit the gas. I could not drive fast enough.

The neighborhood was made up of townhouses that all looked alike. They were painted the same color, the roofs were the same color, the landscaped front yards looked alike, and each shared a common wall with their neighbor.

I couldn't see the lake from my car, but as I pulled up, several people ran outside, saw me and pointed inside. I ran through the living room and saw the lake through the open sliding glass doors. A lone man was in the water, and as I ran toward him, he dived and came back up with a panicked look on his face and dived again.

I was waist-deep in water making my way to where I had last seen the man. In South Florida, most of the lakes are actually rock pits developers created for landfill. The lakes are typically forty feet deep, and usually, the drop off from the shoreline is steep.

It was so frustratingly hard to hurry in the water. My heavy boots and bulletproof vest made it even more difficult, and the water seemed as thick as molasses. With the water up to my shoulders, I was about to dive under when the man surfaced, holding a small lifeless girl. He was struggling, probably exhausted, and his head was just above the water. I was barely able to touch the bottom, and I draped her over my shoulder and began wading to the shoreline thirty feet away. It was agonizing, bouncing up and down on the bottom, trying to get her to the shore. I wanted to run, but running was impossible. I should have gone back and checked on the man, too, but my mind was focused on the child.

I had to get her on solid ground if I was going to do CPR. So many thoughts were going through my head: I had been trained for this, and my plan was to start CPR as soon as I reached the shore, but I could hear sirens, lots of them, coming from different directions.

When I reached the shore, I saw the flashing red lights of a fire-rescue truck through the still-open front door, so I changed my mind about starting CPR and began running.

I ran with one arm around her bottom and the other hand on her back through the townhouse. I was soaked and my boots were slipping on the glossy ceramic tile floor; I feared I would fall, and both of us would crash onto the floor.

Her face was next to my ear, and as I ran, I felt her jerk, like a spasm, then felt warm water running down the back of my uniform shirt and under the bulletproof vest. She jerked again and puked up more water. I thought, how much water can such a tiny girl hold? Then she coughed and I felt her take a deep breath.

Fire-rescue took her from me as I reached the front yard and soon I heard her crying. It was a glorious sound, and I choked up. All the family and neighbors around the rescue truck were weeping, too.

I don't remember taking my gun belt off, but I found it on the shore later. I radioed my lieutenant and told him what had happened and drove home to change. I threw my uniform in the washer, bleached the cover of the vest, took a shower, and was back in the city an hour later.

Somehow, the jolting as I ran with her acted like CPR, or the man upstairs was watching over us both. I didn't think or talk about this call for the next several days. There was some uncertainty in my mind I didn't want to deal with yet; did I save her or was I just lucky?

Oddly, there were adults in the front yard screaming and

crying, there were more inside the house and some even in the backyard—but there was only one man in the water looking for her. Any of them could have done what I did.

Today I can still see her lifeless body in the man's arms and feel the sensation she was already dead as I draped her tiny body over my shoulder.

I didn't want to tell my friends or even my wife what had happened; it felt like I was trying to take credit for something that was nothing more than luck, luck and the stranger who pulled her up off the bottom.

Eventually, I started wondering how she was, and would she remember that day?

Now I understand why I was reluctant to talk about it then. I was no hero, I didn't perform any act of heroism, I was simply part of a fortunate series of events.

I'm glad I was in the right place at the right time.

Chapter 39

Do Officers Cry?

My father is the strongest, bravest man I know; so when I hear he struggles in his walker trying to make it from his bed to the bathroom, I choke up. I call it choking up because I'm too embarrassed to admit to crying. I feel my eyes burn, a catch in my throat, my bottom lip quivers, and sometimes there's full-blown sobbing—and I'm okay with that.

It's the other times I worry about, like when my wife reminds me of a call I worked twenty-three years ago when a little girl was bouncing on the bed with her one-year-old sister. Susan and I were telling this story to a friend, and I could feel those same first precursors of tears, and I thought—WTF is wrong with me?

It was 1995, and I was a road patrol sergeant working the day shift. It was busy, and the dispatcher asked me to respond to an unresponsive child; such a clean term—*unresponsive,* isn't it? It usually means dead.

It was a fire-rescue call, and I was asked to assist as there were no fire-rescue units available, so of course I drove as fast as I could safely go. The saying is: "If you wreck and can't get there, you're no good to anyone," and I was pushing those limits.

I pulled up to a small series of duplex apartments and thanked God fire-rescue was right behind me.

All the neighbors were outside in the small parking area watching me as I ran in. I was faster than rescue because I didn't have to carry all the lifesaving equipment they do so I was inside first.

In a small bedroom, maybe the only bedroom in the house, were two twin beds with a two-foot gap between them. I didn't see anything else in the room because my focus was now on the unconscious child on the bed.

A woman in her sixties was yelling in Spanish at a small brown-haired girl, who looked terrified. She was three or four years old, and her eyes darted back and forth between the woman and me. She was sitting on the bed next to the baby, her six-month-old sister.

Fire-rescue rushed in, blocking the door, and I backed away to give them room in the gap between the beds. The old woman, still muttering in Spanish, was forced out of the room by rescue.

I couldn't see fire-rescue working on the baby, but moments later they took her lifeless body out to their truck. There was no need for the gurney behind them, they just scooped the baby up in their arms and carried her outside.

As soon they left the room, the woman returned. This time, probably for my benefit, she yelled in English at the girl. "See what you did this time? This is your fault! You did this!"

I directed the woman out the door and watched as she angrily walked over to the fire-rescue truck.

Once I was alone with the still-terrified little girl, I got down on my knee, and I said, "No matter what you hear, I want you to remember this wasn't your fault."

The girl nodded, and I stayed with her until the fire-rescue guys came back in to check on her.

When they drove away, the baby was still unresponsive.

Weeks later I ran into the same fire-rescue squad, and they said she'd lived, hopefully fully recovered. They said the old woman was a caretaker-neighbor. Over the years, when I think of the old woman, she becomes the bad witch in the *Wizard of Oz* or the old lady on the bike with Toto in the basket.

***

As Susan and I told this story to our friend, I watched the flow of emotions on her face— first fear, then dread and anger, and finally joy when she knew the girl had lived—all while I was trying to control my emotions. This was a bloodlessly clean, unremarkable call, and I worry about this woman reading some of these other stories.

Those were the important memories of that call for me, the ones I remembered, but Susan added a few more.

Susan and I had just passed an adoption procedure, and we had qualified to adopt a child between birth to four years old. We were older than most adoptive parents, we knew it and accepted it, but Susan knew I was worried I might have trouble bonding with a four-year-old. I came home that night and told her what had happened, and that adopting a four-year-old would be fantastic.

I have only a vague memory of that last part, but it's what chokes Susan up. For me, it was kneeling down and talking to that four-year-old as we looked at each other, eye to eye.

I wrote this in a hospital waiting room recently while Susan was in surgery. It's times like this I find myself wallowing in depression—I feel I wear it like a familiar cloak. But while driving home alone later, as I reviewed and edited this story in my head, I found that little girl's face in front of mine, and realized I was smiling.

Chapter 40

Mosquito One and the Blackhawk

The Christmas holidays brought an increase in violent robberies throughout the city, and in the mid-nineties, our department began leasing a Robinson R22 helicopter each December. The helicopter was supposed to assist the officers on the ground, and two of our officers were licensed to fly it. An R22 resembles a Vespa motor scooter with a rotor on top, and we dubbed it Mosquito One.

Officers were encouraged to fly with the pilot for an hour at a time, but there weren't many volunteers. Soon, we sergeants were strongly encouraged to fly in it to show the officers there was nothing to fear inside that little death trap.

But I did fear the thing. First, I knew how to fly a fixed-wing plane. I had several hundred hours of flight time, and I was working on my multi-engine, commercial rating. Worse, I knew how hard it was to control a helicopter; by their very nature, they want to fall apart and crash.

But I got in this helicopter, wondering if it had been built in someone's garage, and we lifted off. I was sure at any moment I would fall out the open door or worse, the pilot would fall out, and I would crash and die in a burning pile of junk.

When a helicopter is moving forward, it flies a lot like an airplane, and the officer let me fly it for about two hours. It wasn't too hard until the pilot said, "Do you want to try and hover?"

"Sure," I said.

We flew to Opa-Locka Airport, and he centered us over a small concrete pad and began the hover. "All yours!" he said.

The first fifteen seconds wasn't too bad, then the wobbling started, and I was sure the blades were going to hit the ground, and we would both die.

It was a great experience, and fortunately, I lived through it.

***

One night I sat in Ranch House having coffee when four U.S. Customs agents walked in and sat at the table next to me. They were the flight crew from Opa-Locka Airport, and I had seen their black and gold Blackhawk helicopter many times at the airport and on television.

We started talking, one thing led to another, and one of them mentioned budget issues had restricted the number of hours they could fly. Their previous routine had included patrolling off the coast, looking for drug-running boats and airplanes, but now they could fly only when other agencies requested them.

As I was a sergeant on the midnight shift I said, "We often need a helicopter in the middle of the night when the county aviation unit shuts down."

"Call us any time," one of them said.

A few weeks later we had a burglary in progress call at Westland Mall. An anonymous caller had seen men on the roof, and we set up a perimeter until our K-9 teams arrived.

It was difficult getting the K-9s and their handlers on the roof, and once they were up there, if they got into trouble, I knew it would be hard for us to get up there and help them. So I asked dispatch to see if the county could send an air unit to assist. The answer was no, and I remembered the Customs' offer.

"Call Customs and see if they can help us," I said.

We had never used Customs, and I'm sure a few of the dispatchers were laughing. Even I didn't think they would really come, but a minute later the dispatcher said their ETA was ten minutes.

It was three in the morning and everything was dead quiet when I saw the tiny navigation lights blinking on the horizon. I told the dispatcher I would mark a landing spot using my blue lights in an open area east of the mall, which was just south of the canal on 16th Avenue.

Blackhawk helicopters are huge, and as it came in, the blast of wind and noise was incredible. It landed next to my patrol car and a couple of the agents got out. I explained we needed eyes on the roof and should the K-9 officers need help, we would need to get more officers up there.

"Okay, climb in, Sergeant!"

I can still feel the rush of excitement as I got in. I had been in the county's Bell Jet Ranger many times, but this was a massive military helicopter. One of the crew helped strap me in behind the pilots and gave me a headset.

Even wearing a headset, I could hear the sharp whine of the turbines as the crewmen talked to each other. When we lifted off, it felt graceful, like sitting in my living room chair, and I watched the ground through the window as they turned on the searchlights. The county helicopters used the Midnight Sun searchlight, and these lights were just as bright.

The Blackhawk pilot had to turn a hundred and eighty

degrees to get back over the mall, and as he did, he flew fifty feet above the ground over several houses. With the searchlights on, I saw the rotor blast ripping small trees out of the ground and landscaping and lawn furniture being thrown everywhere, most of it going into someone's backyard pool.

As it got over the mall, it climbed to one hundred feet and did a slow racetrack pattern over the length of the roof. Each time it got to the far end of the loop, it went back over those same houses, and I watched more plants and furniture fly around like there was a small tornado under us.

I imagined those people asleep in their homes when night suddenly turned into day and the thundering helicopter above them shaking their house apart. I knew there was going to be hell to pay the next day.

We never found any sign of a burglary or anyone on the roof. If we had, I probably would not have been called into the captain's office the next day. But it wasn't too bad. I walked out feeling like I got the better part of the deal. I got an ass-chewing, but I also got paid to fly around in a UH-60 Blackhawk.

We were never allowed to use Customs' helicopter again.

CHAPTER 41

THE EYE

I mentioned once before the humor officers use to deal with the trauma they see every day. There is little humor in the death of a man, and after fifteen years of retirement, I find myself embarrassed when I remember this call.

Late one night, actually early morning, a hit-and-run accident involving a pedestrian was dispatched in my zone. As a patrol sergeant, I always went to anything serious in my zone and even in surrounding zones.

I arrived with other officers and found the victim dead in the middle of the street. There were parts of a car near him, bits of chrome trim, shattered glass, and plastic pieces of headlights, but the car and its driver were gone.

The victim was really torn up, just body parts in a pile. I looked at this mess and noticed one of his eyeballs was down near his knee. The eye was intact, it was looking up at us, the optic nerve was still attached, and it was all resting on the leg of the victim's blue jeans.

It was two in the morning, and we were preserving the scene for an accident investigation officer who was on his way when a field training officer brought his trainee by to experience the scene. I asked her, "Officer, use your investigative skills and tell me the color of this man's eyes."

The officer was young, and I was surprised to see her walk over and kneel next to the body. She looked all around the upper body, then found the eye and stood up.

"His eyes are brown, sir!"

The next day I learned from the AIU officer the man's alcohol level was over .30, more than three times the legal limit to drive. He had probably passed out and was lying in the street when at least one car, and maybe two, ran him over and left him to die.

***

I had twelve or thirteen years of experience by then. I had seen too many bodies and too much death for this scene to affect me other than the gore and that single eye. The gore I can remember even today, the emotions of standing next to a dead man, not so much.

I've never dreamed about this case, or the eye resting so haphazardly, but as I recall the man's gruesome death, I wonder how another person would deal with such a memory, and does it affect me more than I know.

Chapter 42

The Gringo Lawsuit

In the 1980s, there were tensions between our mayor, Raul Martinez, and our unions, the Fraternal Order of Police and the Police Benevolent Association. Many believed it was a result of discrimination by the mayor against the predominantly Anglo leadership of both the police department and our unions.

I've mentioned in this memoir the frustration I felt with my promotion to sergeant and later my inability to transfer out of the patrol division. This was the beginning of what would soon be referred to in the halls of the police station as the Gringo Lawsuit. It was legally called John GERRY, et al., Plaintiffs, v. THE CITY OF HIALEAH, Defendant.

I thought about not including the story of this lawsuit, but it was a contentious period in my career, and the anger still rises today when I allow it. It also created some bad blood between me and my coworkers, which has finally healed over the years.

The circumstances that led to this lawsuit consumed me and destroyed my love of the job for ten years. I still struggle today, wondering where I would be and what my life would be like if not for the Gringo Lawsuit.

This story has no gory or heart-wrenching scenes, but it was an experience many can identify with—the story of David vs. Goliath.

In the mid-eighties I took my first promotional exam and placed somewhere around fifteen out of the eighty officers who took the test. I'm guessing at these numbers as I no longer have any of the documentation to support them. This test and the list of those officers who passed the test was valid for two years, and during those two years, ten officers were promoted to sergeant.

Two years later, armed with the experience from the first test, I took the next one and came out number ten out of another eighty officers. During the life span of this list, the city promoted eight officers, leaving me hanging at number two. But there were several sergeants' positions open when this list expired, and until that last day, I had hoped I would fill one of those openings. I didn't, but I studied harder and came out number nine on the next list.

Like the test before, once this new list was certified, the city immediately promoted Hispanic officers to those two open sergeant positions, positions I again felt were mine. I was frustrated and thought the mayor held those two vacancies open, wanting to fill them with Hispanic officers from the new list.

Just before this newest list was about to expire, Raul Martinez was charged with six counts of felony conspiracy, extortion, and racketeering, and was removed from office by Governor Bob Martinez. Raul Martinez was convicted and sentenced to ten years in prison and replaced by his rival, Julio Martinez. Julio Martinez quickly filled the last several vacancies on the current list and promoted me to sergeant.

In July 1991, Raul Martinez appealed his conviction and was granted a new trial, which resulted in a hung jury. Raul was now out on bond and awaiting the Fed's decision to retry him.

Politically, things got ugly. Raul wanted his job back.

Two of Julio Martinez's supporters found cow's tongues at

their office door, another received a fish head in his mailbox, and severed goats' heads were discovered in a police department parking lot. The city of Hialeah was now 88 percent Hispanic, and these symbols of animal sacrifices and Santeria, an African-American religion that developed in Cuba, were an obvious message of political payback.

Raul was reelected in 1993, and the Feds soon dropped all charges against him.

A third trial, which began April 22, 1996, resulted in an acquittal on one count of extortion and deadlock on five remaining counts.

During the next several years the patterns of discrimination continued, not just against me but several other Anglo officers and sergeants, affecting transfers and promotions. I could have understood being denied promotions or transfers if I had a history as a troublemaker or was an inept sergeant, but I had an unblemished record.

I felt I had done enough time in patrol and was ready to see what else law enforcement had to offer. I put in requests for transfers to the detective bureau, the property room, and narcotics unit when openings came up, only to see junior, less experienced, and sometimes troubled, Hispanic sergeants get the job, so this feeling of being passed over for promotion was frustrating, and I wasn't the only one.

During this same period, I was again left hanging twice on the promotional list for lieutenants. Vacant positions were later filled by Hispanic sergeants.

One day I learned a new African American sergeant with a troubled history was transferred to the property room, and I decided I had had enough. My friend and fellow sergeant John Gerry and I decided to sue for reverse discrimination.

We started with our union, the Police Benevolent Association, and we were told they didn't think we had a case. We spoke with our local union, the Fraternal Order of Police, and they said they couldn't help, either.

We looked through the phone book and picked one of the biggest law firms in Miami and set up a meeting with its senior partners. They had a new attorney who specialized in discrimination, Mike Feiler, and we spent the rest of the day going over the details with him. Eventually, five more sergeants—senior sergeants with unblemished records forced to work the street—joined the suit.

The firm wanted the case, and once the paperwork was filed, the shit hit the fan. A slow fan, because it was taken as a joke by most of the administration, but it built up over the next few years as the suit made its way through the court system.

Several officers known to support the mayor would snicker as I passed them in the halls. Not just a few times, every time. I'm sure those guys standing by the copy machine every day prided themselves on how fast they could change an ink cartridge, while I was out in the street changing magazines in my rifle.

A captain called me into his office one day and said, "Jeff, it would be wise of you to drop this lawsuit. Nothing good will come of this."

"It can't hurt me, Captain," I said.

I wonder if the chief or mayor had him speak to me.

I felt animosity from some coworkers and respect and support from others. I'm sure the ones reading this now know which side they stood on then.

During those years there were several mandated arbitrations where the city refused to negotiate or offered us pennies.

One day I spent seven hours in a chair giving a deposition to the city's private law firm answering personal questions I felt they had no right to ask, matters entirely unrelated to work or to the case. As I sat in that chair some twenty stories up in a downtown Miami high-rise, I watched huge buzzards circling outside. How ironic, I thought.

To most of our administration and a few of my fellow officers, the case was just a nuisance until they realized that all the demands to have the case dismissed had been rejected, and a trial date had been set. Weeks later I was transferred to homicide.

It was a surreal moment walking into that courthouse that first day, and every day that week. This was the federal courthouse in downtown Miami, not the circuit or traffic courthouses I was familiar with. The city's two attorneys and several of their staff wheeled in dozens of big boxes on hand trucks and dollies. They set up dry erase boards and easels with flow charts and diagrams. When our attorney, Mike Feiler, walked in carrying a single box that held several small files I thought, Oh, shit!

But the moment Mike stood up and addressed the jury, he was a different man. I had worried that despite all the phone calls and all the meetings, he wasn't fully prepared, that he would forget essential things, but he dominated the courtroom with facts and figures, leaving the other lawyers looking like amateurs.

The testimonies I heard were equally surreal, fellow officers who'd been called up by the city's attorneys and asked to describe their careers, their lack of seniority, and any reprimands or suspensions.

Eventually, the chief himself testified that it was his decision to promote and transfer officers, not the mayor's. But I still don't believe that. Not long after the trial I had lunch with the chief, several times actually, and although we never talked about the trial, I felt some respect for the man. I think the mayor boxed the chief into a no-win situation.

The trial lasted all week, and closing arguments were scheduled for Monday. That weekend was hell. Were we going to win or lose and what would the job be like if we lost? Could I face those hecklers in the hallway? I don't think I slept at all the entire weekend.

We all walked in Monday morning, and I was expecting the worst. That's the way I am, a pessimist, the glass is half-empty kind of guy. But there were signs that last Friday that the city's private lawyers were nervous; cracks had developed in their case, and they were overheard on the phone, telling someone they could lose.

Our spouses and family members filled the gallery. We took our seats at the table and waited, and waited.

Then, hours later, the jury foreman had a single question for the judge.

Oh shit, I thought again.

"We're not sure how much we're allowed to give Sergeant Shaw for pain and suffering," the foreman said.

I looked over at Susan in the back of the gallery. She had a shocked look on her face, but it was a confident look, and it wasn't long before the jury came out.

On August 7, 2000, roughly four years after we first filed the lawsuit, the jury sided with us and awarded each of us $200,000 plus attorney fees. I was the only one who hadn't waived pain and suffering, and they granted me an additional $10,000. The city also had to pay all the attorneys' fees, which I heard was $400,000 for our attorney and $750,000 for theirs.

The city's attorneys announced their intentions to appeal, and we eventually agreed to sit down and negotiate. It was then our attorney announced John Gerry and I would also be filing a new lawsuit over our promotions to lieutenant. John had been left in the number two spot on the last promotional list, which was filled by a Hispanic officer while the lawsuit was pending. The city wanted to settle this new suit as well. They gave us a generous offer, we signed the agreement, and the case was closed.

As we left the courthouse that final day, United States Federal Court Judge Shelby Highsmith said to John and me, "I'm proud of you guys."

One aspect remains that I still don't understand. During our negotiations for the promotional suit, I told my attorney I didn't want money, I wanted my promotion. I was told the mayor said, "Shaw will never be a lieutenant in Hialeah."

So I never made lieutenant, but I did take the money.

The case was in all the newspapers and on television that night. I had calls at home and at work from people as far away as New York and California, all wanting my advice on their own lawsuits. Days later my fellow sergeant in the lawsuit, Mike Flutie, our attorney Michael Feiler, and I sat down with *Fox News* anchor Catherine Crier for an interview on national television.

> Other events occurred during the years the Gringo Lawsuit was in motion, events I think were related to or in retaliation for the lawsuit. Two of those are detailed below.

Susan's Problems

In 1996 the city announced it was creating a new position at city hall, a records supervisor. The position would have offered a significant increase in pay and benefits for Susan, and she studied hard and took the test. She came out number one on the list.

A few months passed, and they chose the number four person

on the list. They weren't legally bound to explain their reasons to skip her or the other two, but she was my wife—and I had just filed the Gringo Lawsuit.

Shortly after that, the city announced they were going to eliminate the desk sergeant positions and replace them with three civilian supervisors, one for each shift. It would be another significant raise in pay and responsibility, and again Susan studied hard and took the test. She needed to place first so she would have seniority and wouldn't end up working midnights. Once again, she came out number one on the list, which should have assured her she would have seniority over the other two and would be able to choose the better shift.

A year went by, and there were no promotions. In July1997, we adopted our son, Stephen. Susan took time off for maternity leave, and in that first week of her leave, they promoted the two women under her on the list. Had she known, or had they offered, she would have returned to work, and I would have taken time off to be with Stephen.

Susan spoke to her union, who recommended she talk with the Equal Employment Opportunity Commission, which we did. A week went by, and a man knocked on our door and introduced himself as Jimmy Mack.

Jimmy seemed irritated the moment he walked in the door. A minute or two into our conversation, I referred to him as "Jim," and he flew into a rage yelling, "My name is Jimmy!" I thought he was going to walk out the door.

Weeks passed, and Susan returned to work. They promoted her, and as a junior supervisor, she went to the afternoon shift and we received a notice that the EEOC chose not to pursue her case. I was not impressed with the EEOC. In retrospect, we should have bypassed them and filed a separate federal lawsuit.

Susan eventually made her way to the day shift when one of the senior supervisors retired. She took on many of the administrative duties, including the communication department's budget, and all the logistics generally handled by the communication's commander, who was never around.

I think Susan so impressed the chief, one of my adversaries during the trial, that he pushed the mayor to promote her to a command position. But Raul wasn't done punishing me yet, and it never happened.

The Day Off

The department was always short-staffed, and many days we were working below minimum staffing requirements. Some were working on overtime, so getting time off approved was difficult.

Months before my son's first birthday, Susan and I began planning his party. We wanted it to be a big one as he was our only child at the time. Our parents, our extended family, and friends were all planning to attend. I put in a request for that Saturday off months in advance just to ensure I could be there.

The party was set for Saturday, July 25, 1998, and everything was planned—until my day off was canceled.

Earlier that week, at the end of my shift, two other sergeants and our lieutenant were gathered in the roll call room waiting for the officers to come in with their reports. The lieutenant handed me my papers, the ones I submitted months ago, and said my request had been denied. A newly promoted sergeant was transferring to my shift, and he had put in for a week's vacation that included the Saturday of the party.

To me, this was unbelievable. In the past, under similar

circumstances, someone would work overtime to fill this day, or the shift would work one sergeant short as a routine practice.

One of the other sergeants in the room said, "Maybe you'll be sick that day."

The next day after roll call, the lieutenant, one I had worked with as a patrol officer and thought I had a good relationship with, handed me another set of papers. I thought he had changed his mind and was having me fill out new papers for the day off.

"Sergeant Shaw," he said, "you violated departmental policy last night with your statement about calling in sick, you put me on the spot with other sergeants, and I'm issuing you a written reprimand."

I thought he was joking at first, but I looked at the papers and realized he was serious. I wanted to rip up the papers in front of him and throw them in the trash. I had already been seeing a psychiatrist for anger issues related to the lawsuit and this, for me, was a breaking point.

Instead, I numbly signed the papers and walked out.

This lieutenant was one of the officers I had seen climb the ranks effortlessly. He was never a standout officer, never a sergeant I thought of as a great supervisor, and now he was a brand-new lieutenant denying me a day off. Based on time in the department, I was actually senior to him, but a promotional list never died while he was on it.

I stewed over this for a week. Susan and I were able to reschedule the party, and most of those we had invited were able to attend. But I never stopped thinking about those papers, and the rage I felt signing them.

I was at a point in my career where I was eligible for early retirement. I didn't see much of a future for me in Hialeah, and with the Gringo Lawsuit pending, things were getting worse.

A week later I was told to report to the patrol captain. I took a lieutenant with me as a witness and as a union representative, a practice we're entitled to if we're being disciplined.

The captain began reading me the riot act and said I could have been demoted or fired for insubordination.

"I never said I was going to call out sick, Captain," I told him. "That comment was made by another sergeant, but if you want to demote me, go ahead. If you want my resignation just ask for it because I'm ready to quit right now," and I stood up, ready to walk out. I had crossed the point of being in control, and I didn't give a shit what happened next.

I remained in front of his desk, ready to leave. I had worked with these two men for years and respected them, but I'd had it. I was ready to quit, and they knew it. They must have had some respect for me because they changed into my coworkers right then—it was as if they'd taken off their brass administrative hats and put their police officer hats on.

"Sit down, Jeff."

I walked out of the office with an oral reprimand. The written one that would have been in my file forever was shredded—and I never spoke to that first lieutenant again.

***

After the trial was over, I was able to put most of my anger behind me. I was away from those individuals I felt contributed to the discrimination, the chief and I saw each other differently, and I enjoyed the last few years before I retired.

Chapter 43

Homicide

I was transferred from patrol to homicide in June of 2000, three months before the Gringo Lawsuit went to trial. Although I had been on the scenes of many homicides, I had no investigative skills other than what I had learned as a patrol officer and patrol sergeant, and I had just been transferred into the most demanding investigative unit in the department.

Most detectives start out in juvenile, burglary, auto-theft, and other divisions. Many of them loved working in those units and stayed there their entire career, but homicide usually required years of previous investigative experience.

My transfer was different, and was more likely the result of the Gringo Lawsuit, although no one ever acknowledged it as fact.

In the 90s, Hialeah was averaging 28 homicides each year, and it remained that way until I retired three years later. The homicide unit also handled suicides, accidental deaths, suspicious deaths, and industrial deaths. For every homicide, there were two or three other types of deaths, so in just those three years, I saw plenty of death.

In addition to the homicide detectives, I supervised the major crimes unit, also called the crimes person unit. This unit handled all the assaults, batteries, rapes, and even shootings committed by non-family members—everything short of actual death.

Some cases I can recall with extreme clarity, and others were so generic I might confuse them with another similar case. Many of the eighty or so homicides that occurred during those three years I don't remember at all. How is it possible to be in the room with a homicide victim and not remember? It's easy is all I can say. Officers become immune to all the misery and the carnage on most scenes because each one has it. But I've since learned the brain remembers; eventually, those forgotten victims resurface in my dreams.

Every homicide is tragic. It's the taking of someone's life by another. Someone is dead, and they will be dead forever. They will have no more memories, no more birthdays, and they won't wake up tomorrow.

I say this because I often stood over a victim and wondered about their life just before their death. Did they ever think as they were tying their shoelaces that morning, a medical examiner would be untying them later that night? Would they have dressed differently if they knew detectives would be gathering around them in a few hours? Were they a decent person or were they an asshole and was it just a matter of time before they made somebody mad enough to kill them? Or were they just an innocent bystander?

I saw so much death in homicide: people shot up and dead in the street, shot or beaten to death in their homes; shot, beaten, set on fire, or stabbed where they worked or where they ate. Something will spark a memory, and like it or not, I'll relive those gruesome scenes every day.

Last night, as I was taking my boots off, I looked at the deep tread of the sole. It's very similar to the Magnum boots I wore on patrol, and suddenly I saw a man's tooth stuck in the tread. It happened many years ago, but it might as well have been just hours earlier.

For the next half hour, I kept seeing the man on the floor, gagging and jerking as he died. I can see the shattered jeweler's display case and tiny bits of glass mixing in with the expanding pool of the dead man's blood. I can see the duct tape on the jeweler's wrists with bits of skin and hair on the sticky side and his little .38-caliber revolver resting on top of a display of watches.

But as the night wore on, the visions of that scene lessened and I eventually forgot about them.

Chapter 44

The Sword

Two weeks after my transfer, I had my first homicide case. Because it was my first, I chose to be an observer—I was there, deep inside the investigation, but watching experienced detectives investigate. I wanted to learn everything I could. My role then was to assign a lead detective, a crime scene detective, and have the rest of the detectives fill in wherever I needed them.

My lieutenant, an experienced homicide investigator, was also there. He helped me through this case and many more, and I owe him a great deal. I owe the detectives as well because they required little supervision.

Residents of an apartment building were complaining of a foul odor coming from one of the apartments, and a patrol officer was dispatched to check it out.

As he knocked on the door, the officer said he heard a gunshot inside the apartment. He forced his way in and found a man bleeding from a gunshot wound to the head, still breathing, and another body inside a walk-in closet.

I arrived in time to see fire-rescue pumping the still-living man's chest as they wheeled him out on a gurney. I saw the guy's face as they went by. He was a middle-aged man, hair dyed orange, tattooed blue eye shadow, and orange eyebrows.

The wound in his hair looked like it would probably be fatal, but I had no time to check as he rolled past me.

Although I was standing twenty feet from the open front door, the smell was already horrendous—almost at the threshold of what I thought I could endure. I had smelled plenty of decomposing bodies by this time, but this one was sickening. Big black flies surrounded the window frames, but the windows were shut tight. The flies knew what was inside, and so did I.

I was determined not to let my fellow detectives see I was struggling with the smell, so I followed them inside the apartment. The air conditioning was maxed out, and it was cold inside. The living room was dark, lit only by scented candles burning everywhere. There were car air fresheners, too, like the old green pine tree tags people used to hang from their rearview mirrors, scattered all over the apartment in what was obviously an attempt to mask the smell.

I was near gagging by then, but I followed one of the detectives into the bedroom to locate the source of the smell.

Just inside the walk-in closet of the master bedroom was the body of a man lying on the floor. He was faceup but covered in several blankets so only his blackened, decomposing feet were visible. He was huge, probably from bloating, as he had been dead for over a week.

In the corner of this bedroom was what at first glance appeared to be a wooden cane, but it was actually a long sword hidden inside a hollow shaft. It turned out to be the murder weapon. An autopsy later revealed the victim had dozens of wounds; many of them went completely through the man's torso.

A few hours later, the other man was pronounced dead at Jackson Memorial Hospital.

The supposed tradition was to smoke a cigar after a detective's first homicide. The lead detective offered me a Swisher Sweets cigar, and I smoked most of it. The taste in my mouth was almost as bad as the stench inside the apartment.

The same detective invited me to join him at the autopsies for both victims the following day. The autopsies were conducted in the decomp room, which was in a separate building just outside the medical examiner's office, and was used for cases involving decomposed bodies and those with communicable diseases. It had special filters and water systems to protect the environment and to protect the staff of the main building from the stench. I knew this was going to be rough and it was. The autopsies were similar to the one I described earlier, other than the decomposed tissues and organs of the one man, and the smell, of course. On one of the walls was a blue fluorescent light fixture that was sometimes used in restaurants to trap flies, and there were some monster flies buzzing around inside this one.

The investigation revealed the two men were living with the subject's mother, and she did not approve of their homosexual relationship. She died of natural causes just weeks before the homicide occurred.

Through a note the man left before he shot himself, he said his lover had told him, "The bitch can't stop me now, you're all mine." The victim further insulted the man's dead mother, and in a rage, the man stabbed his lover over and over and hid the body in the closet. He must have known it was just a matter of time before the odor would attract attention because he was ready when the police knocked on the door.

This was one of the easier homicides because the suspect had done all the hard work. Most of our job was documenting the scene. I never puked on this case or any other, but some of my colleagues weren't so lucky.

***

At homicide school, I learned it is common to find the victim's body, or at least the victim's face, covered with something. It's an indicator of a close relationship between the victim and the subject and an indicator of shame or remorse. The number of stab wounds is another indicator of an intimate relationship. It takes a great deal of rage to plunge a knife, or in this case a sword, into another human being so many times.

As I write this, I'm recalling the stench and eating a ham sandwich at the same time. I wonder if that's normal or do I have issues I should worry about. I do recall seeing one of the medical examiners doing an autopsy with a Burger King bag next to him, so maybe I'm okay.

Chapter 45

The Suitcase

The woman in the suitcase was one of the harder cases, and one of the first cases that had a profound effect on me while I was in homicide.

In August of 2000, I was driving through the south end of the city when a patrol sergeant asked me on the radio if one of my detectives could help him with a missing person case. The department received many missing person cases every day, and depending on who the missing person was, each one was handled differently. Missing adults were rarely investigated at all unless there were extenuating circumstances.

My detectives were overloaded with cases at the time, and I asked the sergeant to have an officer write a report and forward it to me.

"Jeff, something is really wrong here. You should come take a look," he said.

I knew this sergeant, and I knew he had good instincts, so I headed toward the address and asked one of my detectives to meet me. This detective was not overjoyed at having to stop what he was doing to respond to a missing adult.

The missing woman was a young mother in her late twenties.

She was in the middle of a divorce and shared custody of her twelve-year-old son with her husband, who had custody that weekend. When the weekend was over, the father had dropped him off but the boy found his mother wasn't home. He waited for hours, then went to a neighbor and eventually someone called the police.

We arrived and met with the patrol sergeant who explained he had found the woman's purse, her ID, and car keys on the kitchen counter. Her car was in the parking lot but instead of being in its assigned space near her front door, it was at the far end of the complex. All of these were bad signs, or extenuating circumstances.

In the foyer and small hallway, a ladder, paint cans, brushes, and the smell of fresh paint indicted she or someone had begun painting the walls recently. In the master bedroom we found a pool of drying paint puddled in the carpet at the foot of the bed.

The spilled paint set off my own alarms. It was at least a quarter of a gallon and no one had tried to clean it out of the carpet.

While standing in this bedroom near the puddle, my detective looked down at a small spot on the baseboard, and said, "We need to clear out and get a search warrant; this is a crime scene."

The small spot, not much bigger than an eighth of an inch, was high-velocity blood spatter. Normally when someone cuts themselves and blood drops to the floor, it leaves a certain, easily recognizable, pattern. But if someone was hit with an object like a hammer or a fist, it leaves a completely different pattern.

Several hours later and armed with a search warrant, we re-entered the apartment and began our search in the bedroom. We cut up the carpet at the end of the bed and found the pool of wet paint was hiding blood that had seeped through the carpet and soaked into the padding underneath. It was a lot of blood, and I knew then the chances of finding the woman alive were going to be slim, at best.

At this same time, we heard the husband had returned and was in the parking lot. He had learned through his son his ex was missing and seemed cooperative and concerned. One of the detectives drove him to the station for a voluntary statement.

In most homicides, we started with the people closest to the victim and worked our way out. The husband was at the top of our list, along with whomever the missing woman had been dating. So taking the husband's statement was a priority.

The missing person's case was now a full-blown homicide investigation. The entire homicide team and the major crime detectives were all involved; some were talking to neighbors, some were searching the woman's car, and we had people at her place of employment talking to her coworkers. I helped search for clues inside the apartment.

One of the first things I went through was her photo albums. Happy pictures of a young family during happier times. The woman was a petite, attractive mother, who in the pictures appeared to love her family. I found myself still wishing this woman was okay somewhere, at a relative's house or maybe in an emergency room being treated for an injury.

I opened the top drawer of a dresser. Twenty or thirty tightly wrapped bundles of cloth were neatly lined up by color; all the varying shades of reds were together, the blues, the greens, and so on, like a crafts drawer or the display of cloth in a fabric store, and it took me a second to realize they were panties.

I felt uncomfortable, like a voyeur, staring at the woman's underwear and I knew I was invading a very intimate part of her life.

I must have said something because one of the other detectives told me about a case where many hours were spent investigating a homicide only to find it was a suicide. The medical examiner had found a note hidden in the victim's underwear. There was no note in this case, not in the drawer or anywhere else.

We were also looking for anything that might lead to someone who would want to hurt the woman—a diary, pictures of a new boyfriend, threatening letters from her estranged husband or neighbors, anyone—no one was ruled out on a case like that.

We spent most of the night going through the scene with no new leads, except one of the detectives felt the husband's story didn't add up. First off, he had several long scratches on his face, scratches he said were from working with rose bushes at his brother's house. These scratches weren't claw-like scratches, like injuries from a fight, or we would have keyed in on him sooner.

Several other detectives sat with him and listened to his alibi and agreed that something was odd—his body language and his emotional responses were wrong, not what we would expect from either a concerned husband or from grief.

There was one detective I thought of as a pit bull, and I mean that as a compliment. Ralph was aggressive and once he latched on to something, he would never let go. In homicide, we seldom worked misdemeanors, but every once in a while I had one that needed to be investigated. For example, if I wanted some closure for the victim, I would give the case to him. He never complained, and he would dig through the case, as if it were a homicide, until there was nothing left to find. And if someone needed an introduction into the criminal justice system, Ralph would do it.

He asked me if he could talk to the husband. Ralph was never violent during an interview, never screamed or threatened anyone like on TV, but he had a way about him that got to people—they *wanted* to confess. He spoke to them on their level, like an equal; he picked on their strengths and weaknesses and exploited them. About an hour later the husband told us how he had killed her, at least his version of how it happened.

The husband said he had been trying to reconcile with the victim for months, and she wanted nothing to do with him. She had been seeing someone else and the husband was jealous. He took his son's key to her apartment, or made a copy of it (I heard both versions), and let himself in while she was out on a date.

"I just wanted to look around," he said. "When she came home early, I hid in the closet until I thought she was asleep."

Then he came out of the closet and stood over her. She woke and screamed.

"I just wanted her to stop screaming so we could talk."

He said she wouldn't stop screaming and fought with him. "Then I realized she was at the foot of the bed, covered in blood, and she was dead.

He said he spent the next several hours cleaning what he could and hiding what he couldn't. He put her into the bathtub, washed the blood off her, put her into a large suitcase and carried her outside, put her in the trunk of her own car and drove her somewhere, then dumped her, still inside the suitcase. He refused to tell us where.

"Let the worms eat her," he said.

By now, it was midmorning and we were all still working the different scenes. I responded to the husband's brother's house to serve another search warrant. We found the rose bushes the husband said scratched his face but little else. We went back to the apartment, cut out more of the carpet and used a Sawzall to cut out a section of the wall that contained blood spatter as evidence for trial.

Night came and once it was completely dark, the ID technicians turned off the lights and sprayed Luminol everywhere. Luminol emits a pale blue glow as it reacts with the iron in blood, and the bathroom lit up like a slaughterhouse. We found all the blood evidence the husband had tried to clean. That night the husband also finally told us where he had dumped her body.

An hour or two before dawn, we put him in the back of a detective's car, and he directed us to a lake in a remote area near the Everglades. He said he had put the suitcase into the lake, pushed it out into the middle, and watched it sink. We found the lake easily enough, but it was pitch-black and our flashlights were no help. We waited another several hours for dawn. Some of us tried to catch a few minutes of sleep, as it was now over thirty-six hours since the call had been dispatched and forty-eight hours since most of us had slept.

In the heat of South Florida, a body will float to the surface in one or two days as gases form in the tissues and intestines, and it had been two days since her death. As the sun rose, we saw the suitcase floating about seventy-five yards offshore. The Pembroke Pines dive team responded and brought it to shore. I thought of the bacteria surrounding the suitcase, and I was glad I didn't have to swim out there.

As the medical examiner and a photographer bent over the still-closed suitcase, I thought of the woman smiling in those photographs and tried to picture her inside it. Somewhere in my mind, I held on to the hope she wasn't inside, hoping she was alive and was okay somewhere else, but I knew better. The stench told me.

We formed a semicircle around the suitcase, about six or seven feet away. I could already smell death, and it hit me hard, each and every time. I may have gotten used to it, but the fact the smell was coming from another human being made it psychologically worse.

The examiner opened the suitcase and what was inside was horrifying. The woman now looked more like a giant fish than a human. Her eyes bulged out, her mouth gaped—forced open by her swollen and protruding tongue, and her skin was falling off in big sheets that looked like cream-colored tissue paper. She was neatly folded into a fetal position; her knees and hands were up near her face, which was turned slightly toward us. She was so bloated she took up every square inch of the suitcase. I had to walk away.

***

The victim's mother flew from South America to take custody of her grandson and attend the killer's trial.

During this same time in 2000, six or seven prostitutes were found murdered and dumped in suitcases all over Miami-Dade and Broward counties. A serial killer was at large so when the husband mentioned he had dumped his wife in a suitcase, more alarm bells went off, but it turned out our guy was not involved in those murders.

As I write this, the husband, Silvio Javier Mitsoulis, is serving life in prison. But as I mentioned in a previous case, a life sentence does not always mean a lifetime. He is set to be released in 2046.

He was a cowardly, wimpy-looking guy, and I would be surprised if he lives that long in prison.

Chapter 46

For the Sake of Humanity

I was at the station, sitting in my office, when I heard the alert tone and this next homicide was dispatched.

I arrived in a neighborhood of single family homes, where several patrol officers were already at the front door of the house. The officers told me a woman was dead inside and a neighbor had seen the woman's teenage son running from the house. Patrol and K-9 had already set up a perimeter and were searching for him. They looked for hours, going door to door and yard to yard, but the son was gone.

The house was in a nice section of Hialeah, the homes around it were modest but well cared for, the landscaping and lawns were neat and trimmed—a typical neighborhood.

But what was inside the house was bizarre.

The front door opened into the living room and kitchen. Just inside was a simple wooden dining chair surrounded by a carefully organized semicircle of household cleaning products. It looked staged, like a religious shrine. Mixed in with this display was a puddle of vomit.

A few feet away, on the floor next to the dining table, a woman was lying in a pool of her own blood. She had been stabbed several dozen times, bloody footprints were everywhere, and I knew I would have to leave my work boots in the garage again.

The victim was on her back and her wounds all looked similar, except one. The others had bled significantly, but there was one deep gash on her calf that had no blood around it at all. This wound was made post-mortem, after death. It looked as if somebody had knelt down and purposely sliced open the dead woman's calf—which was exactly what had happened.

All night and several hours into the next day we searched for the victim's son. We had missed him several times as he and his friends hopscotched all over Dade and Broward County trying to find a place to hide.

Just before noon the next day, we received a phone call from one of the subject's friends, saying they had talked him into surrendering and were all on their way to our station. They never made it. Fearing he would change his mind, we kept looking for him and found them as their car came back into the city.

His confession was as bizarre as the crime scene.

His mother and father had divorced when he was in his early teens. When he was fourteen, his mother began dating another man who didn't like the son, so his mother kicked her only child out into the streets. For years he was either homeless or living with friends.

The mother and boyfriend eventually broke up and she called her son. "Too much time has passed and I want to see you. Come home for dinner and we can talk."

The kid owned a large ornamental knife; it was junk really, like a prop in an *Aladdin* movie, his friends would later tell us. He carefully slid the knife into his pants and one of his friends drove him to his mother's house.

He said he waited for her to sit down at the table then plunged the knife into her repeatedly until she was dead.

He told us, "I felt the power of Satan" as he stood over her dead body.

Then he knelt down and sliced open her calf.

"I needed her fresh blood on the knife to mix with mine."

His intention was to kill himself by plunging the bloody knife into his heart so he could "join the army of Satan."

But he chickened out. We saw a small nick on his chest where he said he had attempted to kill himself.

"For the sake of humanity, I just couldn't do it."

Unable to kill himself with the knife, he decided to use poison. He collected all the cleaning chemicals he could find and set them out in front of the chair, sat down and tried to drink them one at a time. But he vomited and soon realized he was not going to die.

He sat at the detective's desk, shaking with frustration as he confessed. It was hard to watch and hard to listen to but also so fascinating I couldn't walk away. In a way, I felt sorry for this kid; after all, he was only fourteen when his mother threw him out of the house just so she could date another man.

He said he tossed the knife into a lake in Miramar, and we sent divers out but never found it. The case went to court sometime after I retired, and I never heard what happened to him.

CHAPTER 47

LIPSTICK

One afternoon we were sent to a rundown section of south Hialeah to investigate a possible homicide at a seedy motel, one that promised privacy for its patrons—it was a sex motel.

The motel's maid was our complainant. She told us she was doing the morning housekeeping rounds. The door to one of the rooms was ajar, so she began cleaning the room. When she got to the bathroom, she saw a naked man on the shower floor, dead, and called police.

I looked through the glass shower doors at the victim. He was middle-aged, forty, and overweight. His pale skin was matted with thick black hair that covered his whole body—and he was wearing bright red lipstick. The lipstick was smeared, as if he had been kissing someone before he collapsed.

There were no obvious signs of foul play on the body or in the room: no blood, no stab wounds or bullet holes, and no bruising.

The lobby had a video of the victim and a woman checking in, and we recognized the woman as a local prostitute. After a short search we found her, and she admitted having been with the victim.

"He likes to wear lipstick," she said. "We were having sex in the shower and he just fell. I knew he was dead and I was afraid so I left."

The medical examiner determined the man had died of a heart attack.

I'm glad I wasn't the one who presented the death notification to his wife.

CHAPTER 48

THE JEWELER

A patrol officer was dispatched to an auto impound lot where towed cars were brought in by various police agencies and held until an owner picked them up. An employee had noticed a foul smell coming from the trunk of one of the cars and called the police.

This car had been towed to the lot at least a week earlier when the Florida Highway Patrol found it abandoned on the side of the road in Miami-Dade County. When the patrol officer arrived, the employee pried open the trunk and they found a dead man inside.

I arrived in the late afternoon with other detectives, and it was clear the man had been inside this trunk for days. It's hot in South Florida, and the temperature inside a car's trunk can easily reach 140 degrees.

In all homicides, the medical examiner, the state's attorney, and our crime scene unit were notified, and unlike what happens on television, they didn't always respond within minutes. It was usually an hour or more before everyone showed up.

Once the ME saw the condition of the victim, he didn't want to touch anything. He wanted the whole car towed to his office for the examination. We couldn't just reach in and pull the victim out, he was way beyond that.

We followed a flatbed wrecker with the car on top and the victim still inside the trunk to the medical examiner's office. The car was off-loaded into a garage used just for this purpose.

By the time we arrived the sun had set, but it was still hot in the uninsulated garage. Once the car was inside, they closed the big overhead door and we were surrounded by the stench.

The examiner slowly began documenting everything in the trunk, a process similar to peeling an onion—one layer at a time. The smell was really bad; putrid is a good word to describe it. The man was partially skeletonized, and his flesh had turned into liquid that had pooled in the bottom of the trunk. We broke out our little white masks that do nothing for the smell. What they actually did was hold a dab of Vicks vapor rub near our nose and *that* helped with the smell. The smell was so bad even the examiner had had enough. He opened the big doors to air out the garage but soon residents in a condo downwind complained about the smell and the doors were closed again.

Hours later, the man and his clothes had been completely removed from the trunk. Then our investigation began. We found a driver's license and the car's registration in the man's wallet. He was still a John Doe at that moment because it was impossible to ID him from his driver's license photo. One of the detectives and I drove to the apartment on the license and searched for clues. We didn't find much, but it was enough. We learned the man sold jewelry out of his car, cheap stuff like thin gold chain by the foot, and his neighbors told us he sold them to the waitresses and B-Girls at the local bars in Hialeah. We had already found several receipts in his wallet from different bars in Hialeah.

A B-Girl was a young woman who was employed by the bar. Her job was to befriend lonely customers, who in turn bought the girls expensive drinks, hoping the girls would go home with them. But the drinks were actually just water, and the girl and the bar owner would split the profits.

We found a bar where the victim had recently sold a necklace and interviewed a few of the B-Girls. One of them confessed to being involved in the man's death.

The woman and her boyfriend, Rogue Calafell, were in the country illegally. They were desperate for money and wanted fake social security numbers so they could find better jobs. The woman said the victim wanted to sleep with her, and he offered to help her in return for sex.

She lured the victim to her apartment where the boyfriend, waiting inside, bludgeoned him to death with a crowbar. They hogtied him, stuffed him into the trunk of his own car, and ditched the car on the side of a road.

The girlfriend took a plea offer and was sentenced to fifteen years in prison.

We looked for the boyfriend for days only to learn he had fled to his native country, Argentina, and because Florida has the death penalty, Argentina refused to extradite him.

Arrest warrants were issued for the boyfriend, and in 2012, nine years after I retired, Calafell was finally extradited. In 2015 he was sentenced to life in prison and remains there today.

CHAPTER 49

THE POOL

I remember when I was transferred to homicide, and they issued me a beeper and a cell phone. I felt pretty important. But that beeper became a curse. I could never turn it off, I was always on call, and it never failed to go off at the most inconvenient times.

My beeper went off at home and woke me up, another homicide.

It was midnight when I arrived at a single family home in a residential neighborhood. The house looked abandoned, or at least it had seen better days. The backyard was dark; there was no electricity, so all we had were our flashlights. The yard was strewn with junk and construction debris everywhere, including in an unfinished below-ground pool. The excavation for the pool had never been filled in, exposing all the piping for the pump and drains, and it looked like it had been that way for years.

The pool was full of rainwater, a brownish-green soup so thick the beam of my flashlight only penetrated a few inches. All the junk in the pool was coated in the same brown-green algae, and it stank as bad as it looked. I was shining the beam of my flashlight on the junk when I spotted the body. It was coated in the slimy algae, camouflaged in all the debris floating nearby.

The man was facedown and so bloated his shirt and pants seemed they might burst.

I noticed something odd and walked around the pool to get a closer look at the victim's head. At first I thought the man had an Afro and his hair was moving in the water, then I realized his head and his entire body were vibrating—like static electricity was causing his hair to stand on end and wiggle.

Wiggle was the correct word. Attached to every square inch of the victim's body, including his clothing, were thousands of big gray tadpoles—feasting on him.

The medical examiner arrived and eventually pulled the man out of the water with a grappling hook. An employee of the city water department brought a gas-powered water pump to drain the pool water into the lawn and the stench got worse. It probably stunk up the neighborhood for weeks.

We located a witness who said three men, including the victim, were fighting several days earlier. The victim had flirted with a girl who lived next door, and the girl's boyfriend and another man confronted him. They fought and the boyfriend punched the victim, knocking him into the pool.

We found the boyfriend a few hours later, and he admitted to fighting with the man. However, he said when he walked away the victim was alive and well, standing in the pool, cursing at him.

We arrested the boyfriend a few days later when the medical examiner determined the victim had died of blunt trauma to the head.

This case went to trial after I retired and I never learned its outcome.

Chapter 50

Two Men in a Van

Two men were found burned up in a van. I looked back at this case as I was writing it down and I was confused. Usually I can close my eyes and I am back at the scene. The smells, the sounds, the emotions—they are all right there. But other than seeing their bodies in an embrace, like lovers hugging each other, I couldn't remember any of the other senses that should have accompanied the image.

Then it dawned on me, I was on vacation and the investigation was just concluding when I returned. I had seen the crime scene photos, read all of the statements, and sat in on some of the interviews, but I had never been to the actual crime scene.

The mother of one victim sat in my office one day and explained that she knew her son was involved in something illegal and had warned him many times of the dangers. She was very emotional, despondent and crying one moment and angry the next.

To make a long story short, two cousins had been shot and killed, placed into the back of their van, and the van was set on fire. It was a drug deal that had gone bad.

The lead detective arrested two men and charged them with homicide.

Chapter 51

Wynken, Blynken, and Nod

It was never good news when my city-issued beeper went off before my alarm clock.

The homicide occurred off Okeechobee Road in a trailer park called Wynken, Blynken, and Nod. It was a large, run-down park occupied by low-income, mostly Hispanic, families.

I arrived and found several patrol officers setting up crime scene tape around a body in the grass between two trailers. The victim was a young man in his late twenties; he was lying on his back and there was a bullet hole in his chest.

A witness, a friend of the victim, said he and several friends had been out drinking at a local bar when the victim and one of the other men argued over a woman. The argument continued as they drove back to the trailer park and as soon as they got out of the car, the man shot the victim point-blank.

The witness said the gunman stood over the victim and said in Spanish, "Take a bullet like a man," then fled in his Ford Explorer.

The witness said he kneeled over his friend, who said, "I did it! I took a bullet like a man!" then died.

We had the suspect's name and even the type of vehicle.

A computer search of the suspect's name gave us his driver's license information, including his home address in Tampa. We notified Tampa police to be on the lookout for the subject and his car, and an hour later Tampa told us the Explorer was parked in front of a trailer in their jurisdiction.

We raced to the west coast down I-75 at speeds I can't mention, trying to arrive before their SWAT team made the arrest. We wanted custody of the man; we wanted to interview him before Tampa intervened, which would complicate our investigation and involve Tampa's court system, leading to a jurisdiction nightmare.

We arrived just in time to see the team's entrance. Our man didn't resist and the Tampa Police Department transported him to their station. Fortunately, they were more than eager to be rid of this man and allowed us to take full custody.

I sat in on the suspect's interview with our detectives. The man was proud of his actions. He told us he had spent most of his life in Cuban prisons, dealing with the Cuban police, and he wasn't afraid of us or any American prison.

There is the clichéd phrase, *his eyes were cold and empty,* and this man's eyes were just that—cold and empty. The eyes of sharks and psychopaths.

Only a desk separated us, and I felt he could leap across the desk at any time and take us on. I wished he would.

He was sentenced to life in prison.

Chapter 52

Doctor Emma

I used to have a problem with wounds, specifically lacerations. Strangely, gunshot wounds have no effect on me; however, lacerations, especially my own, make me queasy. As a kid, I would sometimes pass out, and on this night it almost happened again. This homicide occurred in the same trailer park just weeks after the one in the preceding chapter.

Patrol officers had been dispatched to the Wynken, Blynken, and Nod trailer park to investigate a disturbance between neighbors and found an unresponsive victim inside one of the bedrooms. Once he was confirmed dead, they cleared the trailer and alerted communications.

I got the phone call at home in the middle of the night. I had the dispatcher call all the homicide detectives and several of the major crime detectives to meet me at the trailer.

When I arrived a group of patrol officers and my detectives were waiting outside; none of them were happy. It had been a busy few months in homicide and my detectives were overloaded. Most had worked all day, and I knew they were preparing for upcoming trials. We were waiting for the search warrant to begin the investigation.

In most homicides, the initial investigation began once we knew the warrant had been signed and was en route to the scene. It usually required a phone call to the state's attorney and even in the middle of the night, took less than an hour.

Meanwhile, we interviewed witnesses and we learned from the complainant, who was a friend and neighbor of the dead man, that this victim had recently argued with a neighbor down the street. It seemed like an easy case so I assigned this murder to a major crimes investigator instead of one of my homicide detectives.

The detective was thorough. I liked his work, and I wanted to give him a chance and some experience in homicide. The investigation of an average homicide was not much different from what he was used to, so I thought it was a win-win decision, and I was not disappointed.

The detective was grateful, but my captain was not.

As usual, the body was left undisturbed until the medical examiner arrived. When the ME arrived, a petite Vietnamese woman I had worked with in the past, I went inside the trailer with her as the detectives fanned out to locate more witnesses.

The examiner was very quiet and very meticulous, taking photographs, measuring things like the length and width of the room, the size of the bed, the furnishings and their distances from the victim's body. I was the only one in the room with her at that moment, and she asked me to shine my flashlight on the man's head.

My Streamlight lit up the entire room, and I got my first real look at the victim.

He was half-sitting, half-leaning against the wall and the dresser with his head facing down. He was about thirty years old and had jet black hair. The wound was right on top of his head; his hair was matted with blood and torn away from his skull, which was shattered, like a broken egg, with concentric rings radiating out from the center.

The doctor took something, maybe a pen, and started prodding the pieces of bone, making wet, squishy noises. She lifted a section of the skull and exposed the man's brain.

Although I was feeling a little weak, I knew I couldn't pass out in front of this woman. I would never live down the humiliation.

"Sergeant, the light, please."

I looked down, and the beam of my flashlight had drifted away from the wound and was now illuminating the floor. The doctor was staring up at me with what might have been a slight grin. *She knows!*

My knees were weak and I was lightheaded. I bit down hard on my lip, tightened my abs until they hurt, and made it through the rest of the examination, thank God.

After a short search, we arrested a neighbor in the trailer park who confessed he wanted something the victim owned enough to kill him with a hammer. Another typical homicide; no grieving family, neighbors, or friends this time.

***

Although every death had some effect on me, this one was minimal. The long-term effect was probably not grief for the victim, but the sadness in knowing how cheap and meaningless life is to so many people—or at least to the people I dealt with every day.

The lead detective on this case remained in major crimes until an opening in homicide became available and he was transferred. He went on to finish his career in homicide handling several dozen homicides of his own. He is now a successful private investigator.

Chapter 53

I Don't Love You Anymore

I was on my way to lunch when I was called to the scene of a homicide.

An SUV was parked at the curb of a small strip mall. Inside the SUV a man and a woman in their early or mid-twenties were in the front seat. The man was behind the wheel and both were dead from gunshot wounds. On the passenger side floorboard was an automatic pistol.

The man had two gunshot wounds, one to the chest and one to the head. The woman had a single, self-inflicted gunshot wound to her right temple.

Looking inside the car, the evidence told the story. It was difficult, but not impossible, for a man to shoot himself twice, and equally difficult but not impossible for him to have shot his passenger in the right side of her head first. But the blood spatter, bullet trajectories, and interviews with family told us all we needed to know.

The man had recently broken up with the woman. She arranged a private meeting as an attempt to get back together. When he refused to resume the relationship, she shot him and turned the gun on herself.

I had no involvement in the ensuing investigation, which was quick. The scene was fresh, the blood was still wet, and I wasn't sure why I felt so detached, other than as a supervisor, I had little to supervise. The crime scene units came out, the medical examiner arrived, I watched them all, then I left to eat lunch.

***

I used to walk away with some empathy for the victims but not these two, at least not then. Today, it depresses me, although not as much as some of the others. I still wonder what was so wrong with this woman that she had to kill a man she claimed she loved, then end her own life as the answer to her problem.

Chapter 54

I'll Be Waiting for You

The term "domestic violence" doesn't do this case justice.

A young woman and her husband were in their apartment. The wife supposedly insulted her husband, and he stabbed her in the chest with a big chef's knife.

After stabbing her, he sat down at the kitchen table and called the police. "I just killed my wife," he said. "I'll be waiting for you."

The first patrol officers arrived, and sure enough, the guy was sitting at the table, smoking a cigarette, with his dead wife at his feet.

When I arrived, the guy was in handcuffs, standing in the hallway. He was big—over six feet tall and at least 250 pounds. He looked dazed, and he wouldn't look at or acknowledge anyone. Maybe he saw his future—in prison for the rest of his life.

I walked to the dining area and looked at his wife on the floor. She was lying on her side facing away from us and her long brown hair covered her face. Underneath her was a large pool of blood.

She was wearing skinny jeans and a black top and was really

thin, anorexic thin, and was barely five feet tall and probably weighed less than ninety pounds.

The husband showed no remorse, no emotion at all. There was little to investigate on this case. Most of our time was spent documenting the scene.

The husband was charged with second-degree murder. I didn't sit in on the confession, and I don't know for sure if he ever gave one, other than what he said on the phone.

I never went to his trial. In fact, many of these cases never go to trial. The defendant often accepts a plea from the state's attorney to avoid the death penalty or life in prison, and second-degree murder is usually less than a life sentence.

There was a coldness about this man—not the evil I felt from the psychopath in the trailer park case, but cold, as if the man had detached himself from any emotions one would expect after killing a spouse—or killing anyone.

I've seen so many people's reactions after committing horrible crimes. Usually I saw some form of remorse or guilt, sometimes the frustration of having been caught, but this man was a blank page: no rage, no regrets, just the look of a man who had completed one chore and was ready to move on to the next.

Maybe that's another sign of a psychopath.

Chapter 55

The Ñeta

This case began with a 911 phone call—a civilian saw a driver smoking marijuana while driving through Hialeah. The caller provided a tag number and the dispatcher discovered the car had been reported stolen. A BOLO, be on the lookout, was issued and an officer picked up the car and radioed for backup. Once the backup was in the area they tried to stop the car, but the driver fled with the officers in pursuit.

It was January 2002, and my beeper goes off at two in the morning; it was one of our communications supervisors.

"Sarge, it's Ellie ***. Officer Frank **** just shot and killed an unarmed auto thief, do you want to respond?"

It took a few seconds for the cobwebs to clear and for her words to sink in. *Shit,* I thought, an unarmed auto thief. "I'll be right there."

I arrived in a high density, townhome-apartment neighborhood with a real gang problem, the same neighborhood where the quinceañera shooting occurred.

The victim was lying facedown on the asphalt street with two bullet holes in his back. He was not wearing a shirt, and the bullet holes were hard to miss. A stolen car was parked just a few feet away and two marked police cars were parked just behind it.

A large crowd had lined both sides of the street, and in the crowd were some of the local gang members, and they were angry. Some of them knew the victim and were crying, but most of them were threatening, taunting us, and I sensed the scene could get out of control quickly. We brought in extra uniformed officers for crowd control, and soon most of the night shift was lining the street.

A patrol sergeant filled me in on the events prior to the shooting. An officer had picked up the stolen car driving through the city and requested a backup officer. When the two officers tried to stop the car, the driver took off at high speeds and eventually bailed out on foot.

One of the officers fired his shotgun at the man. The other officer heard the shotgun blast and fired his handgun, striking the victim twice in the back, who dropped and died instantly.

The officer with the shotgun was using a "less lethal" shotgun. It was identical to all the other shotguns we used, but it was painted bright red and was loaded with bean bag ammunition.

The bean bag was designed to knock someone down without serious injury, and officers are trained to yell "less lethal!" prior to firing to avoid this exact situation. The first officer swore he did and the other officer swore he didn't hear it.

Because this was a police-involved shooting, every member of our administration, each city politician, and the state attorney's office and the medical examiner's office were notified.

At two in the morning it took hours for everyone to assemble. The victim's body lay in the street until several hours after sunrise and by then there were also a half dozen news vans and reporters all wanting statements. It was a circus.

The victim's friends and family were outraged he was still lying in the street. They didn't understand or didn't care about the forensic details that had to be documented before the body was moved.

Crowd control was also becoming a problem once the sun rose. Our perimeter and the media trucks were creating traffic jams just as people needed to leave for work. Politicians were giving interviews, and the victim's friends were also giving interviews, which created another nightmare as we tried to dispel false information. With all the eyewitnesses who claimed to be present, one would have thought a major rock concert was being held in the parking lot at the time of the shooting.

The victim was a member of a prison gang known for violence, the Ñetas, and the name was tattooed in huge letters across his torso. We expected retaliation from this gang but it never came.

The officer who fired the shots that killed the man was suspended with pay, pending a decision by the state's attorney. The SAO sat on this case for nearly a year before declining to prosecute. The officer returned to full duty.

Chapter 56

The Pirate

On Monday, July 23, 2001, I was sitting at my desk going through reports when a shooting was dispatched on the radio. The call was just a few blocks from the station and several detectives and I got in our cars and raced to the scene.

As I negotiated my way around the red light in front of the station, I rear-ended the detective in front of me. It was just an embarrassing dent, so we kept going.

We arrived at a small house on a corner lot where the victim was sitting in a chair on the front porch. She was slumped forward, and I couldn't see her face but I did see a ragged bullet hole in the top of her head. Blood was still draining off her head, onto her lap, and into a huge pool on the porch.

We learned from neighbors the dead woman was Elizabeth Vega. She and her husband, Alex Quevedo, had arrived in the U.S. from Cuba three months earlier and had just separated in June.

Her husband had come to the house and an argument ensued. As she sat in the chair, he fired two bullets straight down into the top of her head, killing her instantly. After killing her, the husband dropped their four-year-old daughter off at a nearby house and fled. We looked for him all night until we ran out of leads and had to quit.

The next day we were in the office going over the case when we heard about a boat hijacking in Key West on live TV. We watched as Monroe County's SWAT team had a standoff with the hijacker. The reporter said the hijacker's name was Alex Quevedo, and he was eventually shot. However, he managed to survive being shot in the chest with a .308-caliber sniper rifle, which I still find extraordinary.

Quevedo had fled Hialeah to the Florida Keys, hoping to commandeer a boat big enough to get him back to his home in Cuba. But the boat got stuck in the mud, which initiated the SWAT standoff.

In 2008, Quevedo was sentenced to life in prison.

I received a day off without pay for damaging my car. I looked at it as a business expense, and I probably needed the day off anyway.

CHAPTER 57

KENT

The Routine Domestic

Just a routine domestic, right?

In the academy they told me more officers were killed during domestic calls than any other and to never assume one was going to be routine.

One night I was working in the north end of Hialeah when I heard my friend, Kent, dispatched to a routine domestic dispute in the south end of the city.

It was routine until I heard Kent scream, "Shots fired!"

I raced to the scene and listened to the radio as I drove. I knew Kent was okay but someone else was down. Someone else was dead.

I arrived and saw the dead man was in the parking lot, officers had secured the perimeter, and the domestic dispute was no longer an issue. My friend, though, was not secure, and he was not okay. He was clearly hyped-up and suffering the aftereffects of having just killed a man.

I saw Kent suffering what I had suffered myself just a few months earlier when I had fired my weapon. He was wound up like a child's toy that had been wound one crank too many times. Everyone was busy, but Kent had nothing to do.

Remembering the advice my friends and union attorneys gave me when I fired my weapon at someone, *Don't talk to anyone until you have legal representation,* I sat him in the front seat of my patrol car to keep him away from his other friends and coworkers.

Anything we said, even to our best friends, became etched in stone and could come back to haunt us later in a criminal or civil trial. For people who aren't police officers, this may sound almost criminal in itself. Why would speaking the truth be a bad thing?

In the chapter, "The Next Two Rounds," I shot at and missed two men that night. I wanted to tell everyone what had happened and why I had fired. But the truth was and is—officers can be so traumatized, so enveloped by tunnel vision—we can't remember it all. It takes hours or days before all the parts start coming back together. Then the memory becomes a cohesive story, and we remember exactly how it happened.

Defense lawyers say this is just time to get our lies straight, to conspire with other officers to hide the truth, but I know better. I didn't want Kent to speak to anyone other than his closest friends, who all knew better than to ask, "What happened?"

As it turned out, Kent had just arrived at the domestic when a man in the parking lot, some thirty yards away, fired a shotgun at him. As the pellets sprayed out around Kent, he returned fire—a single shot that hit the man in the forehead, killing him instantly—a good combination of luck and skill with a handgun.

One of the people involved in the original domestic had telephoned their father, and it was the father who was in the parking lot with the shotgun. Why he fired his shotgun at a uniformed officer we will never know.

The Dreadlock

Several years later, I was the homicide sergeant and driving to work along Lejeune Road. I turned on my police radio and found myself listening to a wild car chase with shots being fired.

In the south end of the city, four men in a stolen SUV had begun firing shots randomly at other motorists. Not just one round or two—they were firing a machine gun.

As the calls to communications were coming in, officers found the SUV driving at high speeds and began pursuit. Many more shots were fired, and my friend Kent, now a patrol sergeant, was heading straight into the pursuit. When the SUV tried to cut through a gas station, Kent blocked them off, stepped out of his car, and fired through the SUV's windshield, killing the driver instantly and ending the chase.

When I arrived, all the passengers were in custody, and the driver's body was still behind the wheel. There were two or three bullet holes in the windshield. Inside the car the driver was slumped to his right side, and there was a bullet hole in his forehead and another bullet hole in the driver's headrest. A braided section of hair several inches long, identical to the braids on the driver, protruded from the hole.

On the floorboard behind the driver, the butt end of an Uzi machine gun stuck out from under the seat.

Kent looked at me and shook his head, and this time I knew he was okay.

Officers and crime scene technicians spent hours combing several miles of streets collecting empty shell casing. Somehow, and fortunately, no one else was killed or injured.

Later in the homicide office, the dead driver's family was coming in for interviews, and one of them asked me why we had killed her cousin.

I asked her, "Why was your cousin firing at innocent people and our police officers with an Uzi machine gun?"

I'm sure at one time her cousin was probably a good kid, but not this day.

***

I spoke with Kent recently while I drove home from Atlanta. We talked about our shootings and how they had affected us over the years, comparing notes more or less, and I found myself reliving all three events.

I could hear it in Kent's voice, too. Rapid fire words, spoken too fast and too loud. I had chills, and I could feel my chest tighten as my blood pressure skyrocketed. I had to force myself to slow down and relax. Susan was driving, and I caught her looking at me, probably worried I was getting too deep into memories I should leave alone.

Hopefully Kent will be at our next reunion and we can talk about it all over again. We can relive those exciting but horrible events like they occurred yesterday, when we were still young and fearless.

Chapter 58

The Church and the Mirror

Another suicide and this one was at a church, of all places.

It was the middle of the day when the call was dispatched. One of my detectives and I were on our way to lunch, and we responded.

We found an older man collapsed in front of the church's side door. The man was dead, a gunshot wound to his right temple. Next to his body was a small caliber revolver and hanging from the church's door was a hand mirror.

I turned to the detective and asked, "Do you think he used the mirror because he wanted to see himself die?"

"Probably not. The mirror is a common tool," he said. "The victims want to make sure the gun is lined up correctly to ensure the shot's fatal."

Was this a religious man, I wondered? Did he kill himself at the church hoping God would forgive him for committing suicide or was it just a convenient place?

I learned the man was suffering from a terminal illness and didn't want to be a burden to his wife and family, an all-too-common motive for suicide.

Chapter 59

The Colt 1911

"Sometimes even to live is an act of courage."

— Lucius Annaeus Seneca

Some suicides are worse than others.

A patrol officer was dispatched to a suicide at a medical office building. I was the homicide supervisor and I was nearby, so I drove to the address to assist the dispatched officer.

I had been treated for a back injury in this building several months earlier, and I knew my doctor owned the building.

I arrived before the patrol officer and walked into a large office on the third floor of the four-story building. I saw several women sitting at their desks, sobbing. Others were standing, whispering to each other, then they all stopped and looked at me.

The doctor who treated me for the back injury was also in the room. He was standing beside the door to a smaller office, recognized me and waved me over. I stepped inside the office with the doctor and saw a special kind of horror. I closed the door.

Sitting at his desk was a well-dressed man in his late forties, maybe early fifties. He had black hair with the silver streaks some people find distinguishing.

The office was impressive: beautiful wood bookcases, lined with equally impressive medical journals, rich wood-paneled walls. Paintings and diplomas in beautiful frames were hung everywhere. The dark wood desk alone was worth more than the women outside earned in six months, but it was covered with blood and bits of flesh and bone and it was probably ruined.

In the man's lap was a Colt 1911 .45-caliber automatic pistol, and like most 1911s, its finish was blue steel with wooden grips. It looked new or was in mint condition.

There was an empty cartridge stuck in the gun's ejection port. The jammed cartridge is called an FTE, failure to extract. It's also called a stovepipe because it's black and sooty, just like the flue on an old gas stove.

A stovepipe happens to an automatic when the shooter doesn't have a firm grip on the gun, like if the shooter was holding it backward and unable to wrap his fingers around the grips. The loose grip absorbs the recoil, just like the shock absorbers on a car reduce the jolt when the driver hits a pothole. The weapon requires all of its recoil to eject the fired cartridge and load the new one or it will jam. The gun was also covered in blood.

The man was leaning back in his expensive leather recliner; his head was resting on the bookcase behind him. His eyes were open, as if he were looking up at the ceiling. But his eyes weren't seeing anything; they had already begun to glaze and were lifeless.

This man had shot himself in the mouth, and the bullet exited through the back of his head, along with the gases and pressure that propelled the bullet from the barrel. A .45 creates a lot of pressure, and not all of it can escape along the path of the bullet—

there is just too much. The pressure that couldn't escape blew out from his mouth, causing the mess on his shirt and the desk.

The desk's surface, once neat and orderly, maybe even staged by the victim prior to his death, contained several teeth, along with the other bits of flesh and bone. Evidently, the gun had kicked hard enough to break his teeth loose. A steady stream of blood dripped from the victim's mouth, down his chin, and onto his white dress shirt. I heard each drop as it landed on the mass of coagulated blood in his lap.

My doctor told me the victim had rented the entire third floor of the building from him. The victim, who owned a clinic, had been in financial trouble for months, had been behind on his rent, and had not paid his employees for weeks.

The detective and a patrol officer arrived. I told them what I knew and left the scene.

If I had I taken part in the detective's ensuing investigation, I would have probably learned more about the man, maybe met his wife and children if he had any, and I might have an emotional memory to go along with the vivid picture of the dead man sitting at his desk.

Days later I read the detective's report and signed off on it like I did with the other twenty or thirty reports that day.

***

Other than experiencing the gore of this call, it had no psychological effect on me then. I'm sure I went home that night and remembered this scene as not much different than watching a crime show on television or reading the obituary column. Now, however, I often think of that man's desperation, and of his depression, and how they relate to mine.

Was he weaker than I was, or was he stronger?

Chapter 60

Aging Eyes and My Assault Rifle

In my early forties I started having vision problems that affected my ability to aim my assault rifle, a rifle I used in SWAT and as a member of an active shooter team. There were very few mass shootings during my years in law enforcement, but there had been two horrible shoot-outs, one in North Hollywood, California, and one in Miami in 1986, where officers didn't have adequate firepower to compete with heavily armed criminals. So our department and many others began training patrol officers in the use of long rifles, what we now call assault rifles. I carried a Ruger Mini-14, a smaller version of the military's M-14, and we carried them in the trunks of our patrol cars as a stopgap measure until a SWAT team could respond.

We qualified with these rifles twice a year. During my last qualification, when we went forward to get our scores, my target was clean, not a single hole in it. But the guy next to me had not twenty rounds in his, but forty.

I had fired my entire magazine into someone else's target.

WTF, I thought, and we tried again—same results. Over the years my vision had worsened, and my prescription glasses wouldn't allow me to focus on the rifle's rear sight and the target. I could shoot fine with my pistol because it was held out at arm's length, but the rear sight of my rifle was just inches from my face. That was the last day I carried the assault rifle.

As I re-read and edited the story of the rifle, I realized it was also a turning point in my career. I was getting older, and my age was affecting my performance. I was beginning to see signs I wasn't invulnerable.

This feeling didn't hit me all at once but crept into every aspect of my life. Like a train entering the station, it may be slow, but it would inevitably arrive.

The worst of these feelings happened in my last year, maybe even the last few months before I retired.

One evening our robbery unit needed help in searching for a violent suspect. He was known to be armed and was living in one of the projects just outside of Hialeah, in the county's jurisdiction.

Some people called these projects "ghettos" or "hoods" but we just called them projects, and this was Scott projects, one of the worst.

It was winter, but it was not cold. Winter in South Florida just means the sun sets earlier, and we were walking through this neighborhood in the dark. Most of the street lights didn't work. This was a tough, drug-infested neighborhood with hard-core street gangs who shot out the working lights.

In winter, detectives were required to wear shirts and ties, and I had my black bulletproof vest over my white dress shirt and tie. I felt like a target knocking on doors—in the dark—looking for a heavily armed man.

Years earlier I would probably have loved this moment, but this night I was waiting to hear the gunfire that would end my career earlier than I had planned. I asked one of my detectives to watch my back; I felt as if I was losing or had lost my edge—my survival instincts— and I think he understood.

We knocked on a lot of doors that night, but we didn't find our guy.

Chapter 61

The Feel-Good Moments

So many years have passed. Sometimes it's hard to remember the feel-good moments.

Yes, there were plenty of them, but I don't think they translate into words as deeply or as emotionally as the scene of something horrible and traumatic.

Mom and Dad

I was patrolling one afternoon behind a shopping center in west Hialeah, behind Murphy's department store, and I saw an older couple in their late seventies or early eighties sitting in their car. The car was not in a parking spot but was wedged up at an angle against the wall of Murphy's and was blocking the single lane of traffic. I stopped and asked them if they were okay, or if I could help them somehow.

"I was backing up to leave, and now I'm stuck," the man said.

I could see his dilemma—it was a tight parking space, and now he was in danger of hitting the wall or another parked car.

"Can you help me?" he asked.

I could tell something was wrong right away. I asked him where he was going, and he couldn't answer me. I knew he wasn't just having an issue with parking his car.

I looked over at his wife, who was in the passenger seat. As a kid, I watched *The Andy Griffith Show* every week, and this woman reminded me of Aunt Bee. The woman was sitting quietly in a frumpy Aunt Bee dress, her gray hair pulled back in a bun, smiling.

"What's your name?" she asked.

She thought I was their neighbor from New Jersey who had come to help them. It was apparent both of them were suffering from Alzheimer's or dementia, and I asked the man for his driver's license. He was unable to get the license out of his wallet, so he handed me the whole thing.

In his wallet, I found his name and I had a dispatcher run his driver's license. I also found an emergency contact number for his son, and I asked the dispatcher to call him as well.

"The son is already on his way," the dispatcher said.

The son had called the station to report his parents missing, so I was going to wait for him to arrive.

In the meantime, I figured I would go ahead and move their car as it was blocking the roadway.

I handed the man his wallet and said, "Sir, why don't you sit in my car, and I'll move yours while we wait for your son."

It was too hot for this elderly man to stand in the street, and I didn't want him to wander away. His wife was still sitting in the passenger seat of their car, and I smiled at her as I started to sit down.

I noticed the smell, but it was too late—the seat was soaked in urine. I could feel it soaking through my uniform and into my underwear.

What do I do now?

The man's wife was sitting right next to me, still smiling.

I pretended nothing was wrong and I parked their car next to mine.

The son arrived and promised me his parents would never drive again. I felt his pain and saw the relief in his eyes as he guided them into his car and headed home.

By now I had been standing in urine-soaked clothes for about an hour. I drove home sitting on a towel, showered, put on a new uniform, and went back to work.

I can still see the elderly woman sitting in her son's car, waving to me from the back window.

***

How was this a feel-good moment?

As I get older and closer to the age of that couple, this memory becomes more personal. I can see myself sitting in my car like that one day—confused and vulnerable, and I pray some compassionate police officer shows up to help me.

I've been writing down these memories for several months now, and I had forgotten about this one. It wasn't the urine that helped me remember it; it was the smile on the woman's face as she waved. It was Aunt Bee.

The Follies International

I worked off duty at The Follies International every Thursday night for a year. The Follies was a high-end strip club with lots of high rollers, and the valet lot was often full of exotic cars. I'm sure a few of them were owned by drug dealers.

I was a patrol sergeant at the time, and I had worked other side jobs but this was one of the easier ones. It beat directing traffic in the sun, or worse, in the rain. It beat sitting in a bank for eight hours, and it beat working crowd control at the high school football games.

The worst part of the job was having Big Fannie Annie grab

my crotch every night. It wasn't really a bad thing, it meant she liked me, and it was never sexual, more like a friendly handshake, but one I never returned.

Fannie was the clubs iconic stage performer. Several times each night some poor batchelor would be hauled up on stage and Annie would have her way with him. It was always fun to watch and I still keep in touch with her today.

The club had its own bouncers, so I seldom went out on the main floor. Being out there was awkward. I was in full uniform; the dancers were completely nude and on the tables, so of course, certain parts of them were at eye level.

One night while on duty, I stopped into the club for coffee and to talk with the off duty officer working inside. I parked in the valet section next to a beautiful, bright-yellow Pantera. I love old cars, and although the Pantera was new, it was still pretty cool.

I was drinking coffee with Jim, the other officer, when the manager asked us to keep an eye on his bouncers. Two professional wrestlers were in the audience and had made the fatal mistake of touching a dancer—and the bouncers were going to throw them out.

We stepped out onto the floor and watched. The wrestlers were big and angry, but the bouncers were pretty big too, and although there were threats made back and forth, the two guys left without any violence.

Jim and I went back into the kitchen, and a few minutes later the alert tone sounded on my radio.

The dispatcher asked if any officers were near Okeechobee Road and the Palmetto Expressway and able to respond to a bad accident on the highway.

I told the dispatcher I was on my way.

Fortunately, the yellow Pantera was gone, which made it easier for me to get out of the valet lot. I drove south on the Palmetto, and as I approached the first overpass, I saw some wild skid marks and pieces of yellow fiberglass and sheet metal everywhere. As I came over the top of the overpass, I saw what was left of the Pantera at the bottom, which was not much more than its frame.

The Pantera had rolled over several times and had hit the concrete median. Pieces and parts of the car were everywhere and sitting against the concrete divider were the two wrestlers, laughing.

They were pretty beaten up, with lots of road rash and superficial lacerations, but thankfully in good shape. I talked with them for a few minutes while waiting for the highway patrol to show up and once they did, I left.

***

Other feel-good memories aren't as straightforward; they are often intertwined with traumatic events, like arresting a man after he had brutalized his wife, hearing the clicking sounds the handcuffs made as I tightened them, seeing his face as he realized he was not going to talk his way out of this one. Or arresting a drunk driver after he plowed into a family on their way home from church.

They don't transcribe as colorfully as the gruesome scenes, and they don't stick in my memory as vividly as some of the others. Still, those were the feel-good moments that made the job worth doing.

To be honest, I wish I could remember more of them.

CHAPTER 62

THE BAD EGGS

Every profession has a few bad eggs.

Like doctors—there are good doctors, and there are great doctors. But out there somewhere, the worst doctor in the United States is scrubbing up for surgery. His patient may die or suffer terribly from malpractice, but it won't be on the evening news, and it definitely won't be on CNN— much too dull. It needs to be sensational!

Planes crash all the time, small ones, mostly, but occasionally the big ones go down and kill hundreds of innocent passengers. Months or even years later the investigation comes back—pilot error. There will be no protests, no streets blocked, no riots, and there will be no panel of experts on CNN discussing sweeping changes to the airline industry.

Think about the Lufthansa pilot who committed suicide in 2015 by plunging his plane into the side of a mountain at five hundred miles an hour. He took 149 innocent men, women, and children with him, and the major news organizations stopped coverage twenty-four hours later. Compare that news coverage to the shooting death of Michael Brown in Ferguson, Missouri, just months before.

Back to the bad eggs. The Hialeah PD, of course, had a few of their own. In the twenty-four years I worked there, the department was budgeted for between 300 and 350 sworn police officers and 150 civilians. Of those, occasionally some got in trouble.

The most noteworthy of these cases involved two officers arrested for homicide: Carlos Simone and Richard Caride in February 1985.

Carlos Simone was the type of guy that left me feeling dirty after speaking with him. I worked a different shift than Simone but still came into contact with him often. He would never look me in the eye while we were speaking. Something about him felt dirty—I don't know how else to put it.

Caride, on the other hand, was friendly and meek, almost to a fault. I thought he was a coward or at best, just a waste of a uniform. We often worked the same shift, but in different squads, so he was not a stranger to me.

Caride showed up one day with a new Corvette, then several days later with a new Jaguar. "I didn't like the Corvette and traded it in for the Jag," he said, laughing. He also began wearing expensive jewelry. We had our suspicions but nothing more.

It was still a shock when we heard the news, but it all made sense when we looked back at the signs.

These two officers had been ripping off drug dealers, stealing their cocaine and their cash for months, when one of the dealers recognized them as police officers. So they killed the dealer and his girlfriend—executed them in cold blood. It was a huge embarrassment for all of us and the department.

Caride pled guilty to homicide, and in an outrageous plea deal, received a seven-year sentence in exchange for his testimony against Simone at a separate trial.

Simone was found not guilty at his trial; the jury felt Caride wasn't believable, and I couldn't blame them. The feds re-tried Simone for conspiracy to violate the victims' constitutional rights, and he was found guilty and sentenced to thirty years.

Caride spent three years of his seven-year prison sentence actually in prison. Out of prison he got a job at Miami International Airport and eventually managed the airport's fuel tank farm where he led a conspiracy to steal 4.5 million dollars' worth of jet fuel. He pled guilty, testified against his co-conspirators, and received a four-year prison sentence.

There's plenty of juicy information and a trail of legal battles about the Simone-Caride-Hialeah case on the internet.

***

There were other black eyes for Hialeah—an entire squad of officers was suspected of a rash of burglaries, several others were forced to resign for sexual misconduct, another for money laundering, two for armed robbery, and there were probably a few I missed. But those officers were probably less than one percent of the total number of officers on the department. That leaves ninety-nine percent of the force coming to work every day, protecting people they will never meet, and risking, and losing, their lives.

All for forty to fifty thousand dollars a year.

Chapter 63

September 11, 2001

It was a typical Tuesday morning in homicide. As we did every day, we gathered in the lieutenant's office and drank coffee while we discussed our current cases. The lieutenant or sometimes one of our secretaries would make a pot of Cuban coffee and pass it around to everyone on the second floor.

The television was on, and as usual, we would discuss Robin Meade's wardrobe—and our own. It was a common practice to critique each other's ties or how our socks didn't match our shirts. But mostly we talked about our case files, what we had done, what still needed to be done, and who was going to do it. These sessions started at eight and usually finished right at nine. That morning, I was in my office at nine.

My office was about seven feet square, with a typical office desk, a smaller computer desk behind me, and a television on a stand in front. I was reading reports written by patrol officers from the previous day and assigning them to my detectives when someone walked in and said, "A small plane hit the World Trade Center, turn on your TV."

NBC news anchor Matt Lauer was on the screen saying that indeed a small plane had hit one of the towers. Then came that unforgettable camera view of the gaping hole with smoke and fire coming out of it, and I thought, how could any plane accidentally hit such a massive building in clear blue skies? I had a pilot's license, and it was just too hard to imagine. They zoomed in, and I knew it wasn't a small plane—then the next plane hit.

I can't find adequate words to describe what I was thinking as I watched the debris and the fire raining down from the second building. My brain felt paralyzed—WTF just happened?

I ran back into the lieutenant's office, and we all had the same lost look on our faces. Slowly, the numbness and realization that this was not an accident hit us all and was replaced by anger and horror and helplessness.

Then the Pentagon was hit and finally, the fourth plane crashed in an open field in Pennsylvania. Helplessness was the big emotion. I wanted to grab my gear and race out the door and help—but it was so far away, all we could do was sit and watch it on television.

Not long after the second plane hit the WTC, people began jumping to their deaths from the towers. As we watched the news coverage, we could hear their bodies hit the ground while cameramen were filming inside the lobbies of both towers.

Then both towers fell, one after the other. I knew thousands, and I feared tens of thousands, of people had just died right in front of my eyes. I also knew many of them were first responders, firefighters and police officers just like me, doing what I would have been doing—all of them crushed to death under tons of concrete. In the end, 2,996 innocent people were dead, murdered, while we sat helpless in our offices.

In the next day or two, we lost all hope any would be rescued. During the same two days, we heard New York feared all of their tourist attractions and even the infrastructures were at risk. So many officers had died, and those who were alive were at the scene digging in the rubble looking for their coworkers—New York City needed help.

Soon, police departments from all over the country were sending small caravans to New York, to guard the bridges and tunnels and airports and even the United Nations' building. We wanted to go, too, but our administration was silent. Several of us planned to use our vacation time and drive up there as we couldn't fly. All commercial and civil aviation flights were grounded. Just the thought—the planning and the hope of helping in New York—eased the burden we were all feeling.

This next part I can't verify, I never heard or saw anything to say it was true or not, but I heard the mayor had finally okayed the plans to send a dozen cars and up to twenty officers to New York. I was elated and hoped I would be one of them, and even if not, at least my department *was doing something!*

But the same day, the Miami police were on all the local news channels as several dozen Miami police cars and fire trucks were filmed driving north.

Plans for our trip were canceled. Miami had stolen our mayor's photo op, and he thought his response would look weak compared to theirs.

The feelings of helplessness and anger lasted for months.

One month later Susan and I took a trip to Sea World with the kids. I stood in front of the gates as a massive American flag was waving in the breeze; I fought back tears as I heard it snapping in the wind. It was the same gut-wrenching feeling I had attending the funerals of fallen officers and soldiers—an intense combination of patriotism and grief.

It pains me today that most of society wants to forgive and

forget what happened that day. Almost 3,000 people were dead, murdered while we sat in our homes and offices. More than 6,000 were wounded, and 343 firefighters and 71 police officers died trying to help people they probably never met. And they are still dying today—just from breathing the contaminated dust.

On every anniversary of the attack, I post a picture of the falling man. I wanted to have it here as well but couldn't get copyright permissions.

It's an iconic but controversial picture of a man who chose to leap to his death to avoid dying painfully in the fire he knew would surely kill him.

The picture is controversial because some find it too disturbing or believe that remembering the attack might resurrect the fear and hatred that was directed toward Muslims in the aftermath. "It's politically incorrect," I heard someone say about the photo.

If I were the falling man, I would want people to remember me—to remember how I died and the choice I had to make, and most importantly, the monsters who forced me to make that decision.

As a Christian, I understand I'm supposed to forgive those who do evil, but I have limits. I will never forgive those men or anyone like them. I struggle with my belief sometimes when I wonder why God allows such people to exist.

Chapter 64

The Pulse Night Club

In June 2016, only days after the mass murder at the Pulse night club in Orlando, I wrote an article intending to send it to our local paper as a letter to the editor. As horrific and as traumatic as that night was for the victims and their loved ones, I knew firsthand there would be other victims. I knew how hard it would be on the first responders sent into that scene.

As the days went by I found so much had already been written and shown on television I changed my mind. I didn't want my personal thoughts to be lost along with the thoughts of so many others. I worried my words would seem trivial and even scorned by some readers; after all, people died, others suffered terribly, and the first responders eventually went home.

They went home, unmarked, but I know that most of them will never be the same. Most nights, maybe every night, they will be back inside that club, reliving the horror.

I've placed the article below, and I hope the raw emotion I wrote then is still evident now.

"Gays, Guns, and PTSD"

For most of us, the shock and horror of the massacre in Orlando have dulled over the last couple of days. The mothers, fathers, lovers, and friends of the forty-nine people killed will grieve for years, if not forever, and the fifty-eight nameless wounded will never fully recover.

The LGBT activists will ask for sweeping changes, and the politicians will promise to make them. We've seen it before. People will point to the guns because they are the easiest target, and anyone defending gun ownership will be looked upon as just as evil as the lunatic who pulled the trigger.

Most of the politicians won't mention mental illness or religion as a cause, that would be too costly in votes, but politics is not what I want to write about. I want to write about PTSD, but first, I need to start with gays.

I'm not gay, but people close to me are. I can't fully understand the hardships anyone in the LGBT community faces every day; I'd have to live in their shoes to really know. But I do believe they should have the same hopes and desires to live a full and happy life as I do; after all, it's in the Constitution. All men are created equal—life, liberty, and the pursuit of happiness, etc.

But they are not equal in the eyes of evil people. Every day homosexuals are thrown off buildings, set on fire, beheaded in public, stoned to death, or simply imprisoned in Muslim countries all over the world. Think this is an exaggeration? Google it. Many of these killings are blamed on Islamic extremists, but those countries' governments either support it or turn a blind eye when it happens. And our government gives them millions of dollars so they will be our friends and allies!

I don't think I suffer from PTSD, but I know some of my friends do. They don't admit it, but I can see it. In my law enforcement career, I handled hundreds of deaths: homicides, suicides, car accidents, etc., which was probably an average number for someone working in a city as large as Hialeah.

I can recall every small detail in most of those deaths. Here are a few examples—

I went to an autopsy of a young gay man who threw himself off an eight-story building. The term compound fracture is worse than anyone can imagine. There were so many of these fractures all over this young man—but his face was surprisingly untouched.

He wrote a suicide note stating his lover had left him, and it was too difficult to live without him. So young—I can still see him on the stainless steel gurney as I type this.

As a rookie, one of my first homicides was a shooting at a night club. I arrived alone and found twenty or thirty of the bar's patrons outside. Any one of them could have been the shooter, and I was waiting for that first bullet to hit me.

Inside the bar, I found two people had been shot, and one was still alive. I kneeled over him and told him he was going to be okay. I remember his eyes tracking me as I looked for wounds. I couldn't find any, so I didn't think it was too bad, but his eyes stopped following me, then dilated, and his ragged breathing stopped. He was the first person to die on me. I found out later he had his arms up in surrender when he was shot. A 9mm went in one armpit and out the other, so he never had a chance.

I was going to mention a few more, but this will be the last.

A jewelry store robbery gone bad—I walked in and found the robber on the floor, bleeding badly and jerking the way victims do just before they die. He had been shot in the face by the shop's owner.

The jeweler still had duct tape on his hands, and his little .38 was on the glass countertop. I remember my boots sticking to the tile floor as I walked over to the robber. Thick blood was everywhere. There was nothing I could do for the man and he died before rescue arrived.

Then I noticed a new sound with every footstep, a clicking sound;

something was stuck on the bottom of my boot. I looked and saw a complete tooth, a molar to be exact, was jammed in the tread. That's a pretty gruesome image—a dead man's white tooth stuck in the black treads of my boot.

Here's a tip: before binding someone with duct tape, make sure they don't have a gun in their back pocket.

It's amazing how vivid these memories still are—the smells, the sounds.

So what started this story? I was sitting in front of the TV watching the officers, the crime scene techs, the firefighters, the EMTs, and even the ER doctors and nurses deal with the shootings of more than 100 people, mostly kids, all innocent people except for the (insert adjective here) shooter. I'm sure everyone handles these things differently, but every single one of those first responders will never be the same.

Imagine, the shooting is over, the gunman is dead, and now they have to go inside. They have no choice. I'll bet at least half the victims in there were still alive, begging for help, piled on top of each other, some trying to find their friends. Imagine all the cell phones ringing as family and loved ones began fearing the worst. Those first responders will remember every sound, every smell, every voice, and every face—forever.

Next come the men and women documenting the crime scene. This will take days, and some of the victims may lie inside the club for half that time.

I know that for all I experienced during my 24 years as an officer, it pales in comparison to what those first responders dealt with in just those first 24 hours.

So, as our hearts go out to the LGBT community, our anguish at our politicians, and our hatred for Islamic terrorists—pray too for the men and women dealing with the chaos of that massacre.

***

Since I wrote Gays, Guns, and PTSD, there have been more tragedies, like the ones in Las Vegas and at Marjory Stoneman Douglas High School in Parkland, Florida. Will it ever end? I'm afraid there will be many more to come before my story is complete. I hope I can finish and publish this before the next one—because there will be a next one.

Chapter 65

The End

I was in a suit that last day—I wanted to show you a picture, but I can't find one.

I retired in 2003. Months beforehand, the days were passing too slowly and I thought that big day would never come. Then came the feeling the days were flying by too quickly, and I wasn't ready to leave. Then I felt the anxiety of wondering if I was retiring too early. I could have stayed another year and maxed out my retirement benefits, but I wanted to spend time with my kids, who were still in preschool.

I also knew once that day happened, I would pass from being a senior homicide sergeant to an unemployed civilian. It was a scary time, and I felt depression trying to dampen my excitement.

I remember everything about that last day.

I went to the station that morning to say a few goodbyes to those I knew wouldn't be able to attend the party. I dropped off my take-home car, my radio, and my uniforms, and as I laid them all out on the lieutenant's desk, I knew that I would never see them again. I would never again wear the uniform, and I would never again speak on a police radio.

Then Susan drove me to Tony Romo's where everyone was gathering.

As Susan drove those several miles, I felt like I had been punched in the gut, a nauseous feeling where you know something is wrong, but you can't figure out how to make it right.

I expected twenty or thirty people and I was secretly afraid only a dozen would show up, but when we arrived, the place was packed with at least a hundred of my friends.

The chief was there, and I was glad to see him after all that had happened between us. It was a fantastic party, and I heard and saw things that still choke me up today.

But as I left and Susan drove me home, I felt the anxiety turn to the depression my fellow retirees warned me would happen.

I saw an officer on the side of the road just a mile or so later, and I instinctively checked to see if he was okay, even though I knew I was no longer a member of law enforcement. I was now a stranger on the outside looking in.

I had been a police officer for twenty-four years—and now I wasn't. This may sound trivial, but law enforcement is a way of life, and it felt like someone had cut away part of my soul. I had been somebody with a purpose in life, and now I felt adrift and alone.

That depression lasted most of the next year. It was a mild depression; I didn't go around the house sobbing every day, but the sadness, the separation from law enforcement was always in the back of my mind. I slowly forgot the reasons I wanted to leave the force, which was mostly the politics, and I began to miss the good times that were now over. I knew I would never again sit back with my fellow officers after having just handled a bad call and talk about it. There would be no more war stories to add to my collection.

When I retired, the memories I've shared in this book were always in my head, but I seldom found myself reliving them. I could recall them if I chose to, but for the most part, they left me alone.

Now, however, I find myself sometimes overwhelmed with them. It could be the anticipation of writing them down and reliving them again for this memoir. I know when I'm in the middle of one, I can feel the anxiety build; sometimes there is anger and other times grief, but as I finish one scene and move on to the next, those feelings fade and are replaced with ones from the next story. I've been living this way for two years now, and I'm almost done. I can't wait for that day—to be finished. To bury them and hope the worst of them stay buried.

I'm hoping as the years continue to go by, I can be a better friend to people I haven't met yet, or a better father and husband. I hope I can go to a party and not start profiling the guests. I hope I can relax when my daughter introduces me to her boyfriend. I hope I don't think of something gruesome every time I drive over a railroad track and forget what Susan's saying to me as I do. When she says I'm being too quiet, I hope it's because I'm thinking of something pleasant and not remembering all the times I had to leave my bloody shoes in the garage.

The act of writing, whether it's these stories or some of the fiction I've been crafting, feels like therapy. When I was writing my first science fiction novel, I found myself creating scenes based on some of what I witnessed on the job, which in turn, helped inspire me to write *Who I Am: The Man Behind the Badge*.

I turned 66 recently, and I think of all my friends and coworkers who are gone, not just gone, but dead—some who died in their twenties and thirties. Every year when I go to our retirement reunions I find myself wishing they could be there, too, sharing their old war stories, like we were young again.

I hope that an officer struggling with anxiety and depression like I do will find some solace in my story. I know there is no magic pill you can swallow, no words from a psychiatrist that will relieve you of your nightmares, but you can live. You—and I—have earned the right to feel damaged and scarred. What sane person can experience what we did and not be damaged?

Was my career in law enforcement worth it? Yes, it was. Would I do it again? I want to say no, not in today's environment, but given the chance, and if I were younger, I would. I think it's in my blood, and besides, I know someone has to do it.

My final hope is for those of you who are not in law enforcement, those I tried to protect and defend. I hope the next time you see an officer in trouble on the news, you will also think of all the hundreds of thousands of officers you don't hear about, and I hope you will thank God they are out there right now, doing their job.

And the next time you see a cop in a donut shop, I hope you will wonder what horrific scene he has just witnessed.

Because it's very possible that police officer is *Who I Am*.

EPILOGUE

Photo taken by Janet Shaw Vones

May 28, 2018

Who I Am: The Man Behind the Badge is closer to being finished since I wrote that last paragraph. I've heard from my editor and one of her comments asks how I feel about writing these scenes, and why now. I've been sitting in the dark for two hours now waiting for the sun to rise, and I'm wondering the same thing.

Again, in a way, it feels right—it's a feeling of release and therapy.

I get so frustrated when I hear people bad-mouth the police. I want to stand up and tell them, "Shut the fuck up!"

We average ten law enforcement officials killed in the line of duty each month. Ten people who go to work and never come home, just like Pete and Emilio. And how many are maimed and crippled for life that we will never hear about?

In these last hours before Memorial Day begins, I think of Emilio and Pete, and although they didn't die as veterans in a war overseas—they still died protecting the same people who slander us every day. It depresses me thinking how much life they missed out on. It angers me when I think of the ones who killed them.

I close my eyes and find myself wishing I could go back in time, just fifteen minutes, and save them. To tell Emilio not to answer that call—I'll take it, Emilio. To tell Pete to stand another six inches away from the door. But I can't. All I can do is write about them.

Writing these stories brought some of the memories back to the surface, and it made others that never left clearer, sharper. But I feel confident that when the book is really done, and people are reading it, I will find that these memories have resettled or their sharpness has dulled a little. I hope I'll be wrapped up writing a novel, and I will be living in those characters' lives, even if it's just for a few hours.

To the future!

Acknowledgments

I want to thank the men and women in blue who sacrificed everything, who bled protecting us all and who are serving right now keeping us safe as we sleep.

My wife Susan who has always had my back and kept me focused through dark times.

My brothers and sisters in the Hialeah Police Department who have all shared similar experiences and stayed true to their profession.

My friends that supported me through the years as I've been struggling with this memoir including:

Susan Clotfelter Jimison, nominated for Georgia Author of the Year for *Dear Mark* and *Through the Eyes Of A Tiger: The John Donovan Story*. Susan told me, "If I can do it, you can do it. Write what you know Jeff."

Mari Ann Stefanelli Perusek, my editor and mentor who believed in me and more than once stopped me from giving up.

George Weinstein, another behind the scenes mentor and author of *Hardscrabble Road, Aftermath, Watch What You Say* and several others.

Jedwin Smith, U.S. Marine and Pulitzer Prize nominated war correspondent in Beruit Lebanon. Author of *My Brother's Keeper, Requiem for a Paperweight, I am Isreal, Fatal Treasure* and of the graceful words in the foreword of *Who I Am: The Man Behind the Badge*.

Resources

Badge of Life - Our mission is to educate and train law enforcement about mental health and suicide prevention.

https://badgeoflife.org/

Concerns of Police Survivors (C.O.P.S.) - A national nonprofit organization with the mission of rebuilding shattered lives of survivors and co-workers affected by line-of-duty deaths.

https://www.concernsofpolicesurvivors.org

The First Responders Addiction Treatment (FRAT) - Based at the Livengrin Foundation and founded in 1966 as a nonprofit treatment center in Bensalem, PA

http://www.responderaddiction.com/

Police Officer Assistance Trust (POAT) - Founded under the auspices of the Dade County Association of Chiefs of Police in 1989 as a support organization for the local, state, and federal law enforcement community of Miami-Dade County, Florida to assist officers and their families in times of need.

http://poat.org/

Hope4Blue - Provides aid and assistance to officers whose careers are cut short due to medical injures suffered on the job.

https://hope4blue.org

The Police Wife Life Blog - Supporting life behind the Thin Blue Line

http://www.thepolicewifelifeblog.com

1stHelp - A searchable database dedicated to finding emotional, financial, and spiritual assistance for first responders.

www.1sthelp.net

Drug Rehab.com_- A web resource provided and funded by Advanced Recovery Systems (ARS).

https://www.drugrehab.com/addiction/police/

Suicide.org -24/7 suicide hotlines

suicide.org

Police Benevolent Foundation - Provides financial support for the families of fallen law enforcement officers whose deaths occur in the line of duty.

http://www.pbfi.org/about-us/

About the Author

Photo by Jessie Norman 1986 Florida Police Olympics

Jeff was born and raised in the Miami area of South Florida.

He joined the Hialeah Police Department in 1979 when he was twenty-six and worked for twenty-four years retiring in 2003.

He served in various capacities after graduating from the Miami-Dade Criminal Justice Institute; including road patrol, training advisor, classroom instructor, firearms instructor, special weapons and tactics (SWAT), field training officer, communications sergeant, patrol sergeant, hostage negotiator and homicide supervisor.

He now lives in the North Georgia mountains with his wife Susan.

www.ingramcontent.com/pod-product-compliance
Lightning Source LLC
Chambersburg PA
CBHW030238030426
42336CB00009B/151

* 9 7 8 1 6 3 1 8 3 7 4 7 0 *